THE AUTHORITY OF THE BIBLE

THE AUTHORITY OF THE BIBLE

JACK COTTRELL

BAKER BOOK HOUSE
Grand Rapids, Michigan

Contents

INTRODUCTION

The question of Biblical authority is certainly not a new one. From the earliest centuries of the church there have been periodic attacks on the Bible's integrity, making it necessary long ago to formulate a basic doctrine of Scripture. Thus the material in this book is by no means new, nor is there anything novel about the approach.

We do seem to be living in one of those periods, however, when the attack is being renewed. Even though the issues are the same and have been faced and settled many times before, they are being resurrected again, sometimes in very subtle ways. Hence it is necessary to meet them again and to restate the nature of Biblical authority for the present era.

This book attempts to state the case for the inerrancy of Scripture, which is the only consistent approach to Biblical authority. It is more than a polemic, however. Also discussed are the practical implications of the Bible's authority for Christian faith and life.

The popular style and format will no doubt be irksome to scholars, should they happen to read this book. Such style and format are necessary, however, to make the work accessible to as many readers as possible.

5

1

Jesus and the Bible

Mark 7:9-13; Matthew 12:38-42
Luke 24:44-46; Matthew 4:1-10

"As long as I believe in Jesus, does it matter what I believe about the Bible?"

Many sincere Christians are asking this question today. Some have become skeptical about the Bible's complete trustworthiness. Some want to avoid controversy. Others simply are indifferent to such "dry" doctrinal matters as the nature of the Bible.

Whatever the reason, there are many who would separate faith in Jesus from faith in the Bible. "Faith is directed not to Scripture but to Christ," we are told. We believe in Christ and have accepted Him as our Lord and Savior; why can't we just follow Him? *Does it matter* what we believe about the Bible?

The real question, however, is this: *Did it matter to Jesus?* Was Jesus indifferent toward the nature of the Bible? Or was this a central and crucial point in His teaching? And if it was, what did He teach about the Bible—about its origin, its nature, its authority? These vital questions must be the starting point in this study about the Bible.

Christ's View of the Bible

The Bible that Jesus used was our Old Testament. His use of it was hardly casual or infrequent. His life and teachings were permeated with it; He made constant reference to it. Thus when we read the Gospels, it is not difficult to discern the doctrine of Scripture as taught by Jesus.

Its Divine Origin

Jesus acknowledged the human authors of Scripture such as Moses (John 5:46), Isaiah (Matthew 15:7), and David (Luke 20:42). But He went further. He taught that God himself is the ultimate author of the Bible. True, David wrote Psalm 110, but he did so *by the Holy Spirit* (Mark 12:36). Moses gave the law (John 7:19), but Jesus attributes its words to God himself (Matthew 15:3, 4, quoting Exodus 20:12; 21:17). The words in Genesis 2:24 are the very words of the Creator (Matthew 19:4, 5).

Being of divine origin, the Bible may rightly be called "the Word of God." Jesus used that very phrase for a particular Old Testament passage. He accused the Pharisees of replacing God's commandment in the law of Moses with their own traditions. Thus they were guilty of "invalidating the word of God" (Mark 7:13). But even without that particular phrase, the passages cited in the paragraph above make it clear that Jesus did regard the Old Testament as coming from God.

What Jesus taught regarding the Old Testament He promised concerning the New. On the night of the last supper He told His apostles that the Holy Spirit would aid them when the time came for them to present the gospel. The Spirit would give them an infallible memory and new revelation (John 14:26). He would teach them divine truth, truth from the mind of God himself (John 16:12-15). It is proper to infer that this applies to both their spoken and their written word, the latter being much of the New Testament.

Its Perfect Reliability

Since Jesus regarded the Bible as being the very Word of God, it is not surprising that He affirmed its absolute reliability. If it is God's Word, then it *must* be true: "Thy word is truth" (John 17:17).

Jesus' strongest statement about the complete trustworthiness of the Bible is John 10:35, "The Scripture cannot be broken." Debating with the Jews concerning His own identity, He appealed to Psalm 82:6. He considered the appeal to Scripture as final, since *Scripture cannot be broken:* that is, it cannot be challenged or disproved or denied. It is unalterable and indestructible in its truth. It is *solid.*

Infallible History

It is important to note that Jesus constantly confirmed the historical reliability of the Old Testament. In His teaching He made many references to particular historical characters and events. Assuming that His audience would be familiar with the records, He simply referred to them as factual without once suggesting that they were mythical or inaccurate.

The list of such references is impressive. For example, from the often-challenged period before Abraham, Jesus mentions the creation of man (Matthew 19:4, 5), the murder of Abel (Matthew 23:35), Noah's ark and the flood (Matthew 24:37-39). From the patriarchal period, Abraham, Isaac, and Jacob are mentioned (Matthew 8:11): so are Lot, the destruction of Sodom, and the example of Lot's wife (Luke 17:28-32). The many references to Moses' day include the erection of the brass serpent (John 3:14) and the gift of manna (John 6:49). Events from the time of the kings and prophets include David's eating the shewbread (Matthew 12:3, 4), the queen of Sheba's visit to Solomon (Matthew 12:42), the healing of Naaman the leper (Luke 4:27), and Jonah's ordeal (Matthew 12:40).

These Old Testament characters were not used by Jesus merely as one might use folklore and myth to illustrate great truths. Rather, their factuality is essential to the various points and arguments He drew from them. For instance, the historicity of the creation of Adam and Eve is the basis for Jesus' teaching on marriage (Matthew 19:4-6). The fact that David ate the shewbread is part of Jesus' defense of His own actions (Matthew 12:1-4). Nineveh's actual repentance at Jonah's preaching is presented as a standard by which the unrepentant Jews will be judged (Matthew 12:41).

From these examples it should be clear that Jesus presupposed and reinforced the accuracy of the Old Testament's historical records. Also, His promise of infallible memory to His apostles guaranteed the same reliability for the New Testament (John 14:26).

Infallible Prophecy

Prophecy is another area where Jesus affirmed the full trustworthiness of Scripture. Since Scripture cannot be broken, no prophecy will fail. All prophecies will be fulfilled (Luke 18:31); indeed they *must* be fulfilled (Luke 24:44). A prophecy would not be given if its fulfillment were not inevitable. See Matthew 26:54; Luke 22:37. Jesus said it was foolish not to believe "all that the prophets have spoken" (Luke 24:25; see also John 5:45-47).

Its Absolute Authority

A final point about Jesus' view of Scripture is that He accepted and endorsed its absolute authority. An appeal to Scripture was sufficient to end debate: "Have you never read" what is written in the Bible? (Matthew 21:16, 42; Mark 12:26). "It is written," and that's that! (Matthew 4:4, 7, 10; John 8:17).

Matters of faith or doctrine were established by appeal to the written Word. For instance, Jesus proved the doctrine of the resurrection of the dead by quoting Exodus 3:6 (Luke 20:37, 38). He explained His exalted nature from Psalm 110:1 (Matthew 22:42-45). He taught about His own mission from all parts of the Old Testament (Luke 24:25-27, 44-46). Doctrinal error arises, He said, when Scripture is misunderstood (Matthew 22:29).

This finality of Biblical authority applies to ethics or practice as well as to doctrine. Jesus used Scripture as a norm for conduct when confronted with temptation (Matthew 4:4, 7, 10). He contrasted the solid rock of Biblical commands with fallible human traditions (Matthew 15:3). Even the least commandments are authoritative (Matthew 5:19; 23:23).

Occasionally someone asserts that Jesus challenged the Bible's authority at some points. One writer says the Old Testament was "contradicted or modified by Jesus" in Matthew 5:21-48. This is a remarkable assertion, especially since Jesus prefaced His teaching there by saying that He did not come to abolish the law, that not the smallest letter or stroke would pass away until fulfilled, and that even the least commandment is authoritative (Matthew 5:17-19). He said elsewhere that "it is easier for heaven and earth to pass away than for one stroke of a letter of the Law to fail" (Luke 16:17).

What *was* Jesus doing in Matthew 5:21-48? The same thing He was doing at other times, namely, demolishing the erroneous traditions and rabbinic *interpretations* of the law. See Mark 7:1-13. He was not challenging the law itself, but the way the scribes had taught its application.

What, then, was Jesus' view of Scripture? From the data above it should be clear that to Him it was a book of divine origin, perfect reliability, and absolute authority.

Our View of Christ

When we become Christians, we accept Jesus as our Savior. We trust Him to be able to save us from the consequences of sin. We believe His word that His life was given as a ransom for us, thus removing our guilt (Mark 10:45). We believe His word that He has given us the Holy Spirit to renew our spirits (John 7:37-39). We believe His word that He is the resurrection and the life (John 11:25), and that He is coming again to receive us unto himself (John 14:3).

As Christians we also surrender to Jesus as our Lord. We accept Him as the final authority in our lives (Matthew 28:18). He is always right; we are bound to do whatever He says (Luke 6:46-49).

Surely such commitment to Jesus as Savior and Lord requires us to accept His teaching *on every subject* as true and authoritative. He did, in fact, claim to be the very embodiment of truth (John 14:6; see John 18:37). Are we not bound to accept as true everything He taught about the Bible?

The Alternatives

In light of Jesus' recorded view of the Bible, what alternatives are open to those who cannot or will not accept it? One option is to question the accuracy of the records. One might say, "The Gospel records are simply incorrect. Jesus did not really say those things about the Bible."

This approach, however, has some very serious implications. If the records are wrong at these points, how can we be sure they are correct at other points? If Jesus' statements about the Bible are incorrectly recorded, what about His teachings on salvation and righteousness? What about the record of His miracles, His death and resurrection? One may indeed arbitrarily accept certain parts of the record and reject others. But if one chooses this course, let him be very clear about what he is doing: he establishes himself as lord, and constructs a view of Jesus that simply agrees with his preferences.

But there is another option. One might say, "The records are accurate. Jesus really taught this view of the

Bible. Nevertheless, it is incorrect." One who thus disagrees with Jesus can explain his dissent in either of two ways. First, he may say Jesus was accommodating himself to the popular view of the time, though He himself did not believe it. If that were true, Jesus would be a deceiver. Second, the dissenter may say Jesus was mistaken. If that were true, Jesus would be just another deceived and fallible man—hardly the Savior and Lord described earlier. In either case, if what Jesus taught about the Bible were incorrect, how could we trust anything else He said? Who would He be then, really? Whatever else He might be, He certainly would be an impotent savior and an unworthy lord. But we believe that all He said is true and all He did is right. He is the Savior all-sufficient and the Lord all-powerful.

Consistent Christianity

We cannot evade the question of the nature of the Bible. We cannot be indifferent toward it, in light of Jesus' attention to the subject. Neither can we isolate it from the mainstream of our Christian commitment, since our view of Scripture is inescapably tied to our view of Christ himself.

The only solid option that remains, and the only option that is consistent with full surrender to Jesus as Savior and Lord, is to accept His view of Scripture as the true one.

2

The Purpose of the Bible

Romans 1:18-21; Deuteronomy 5:22;
Jeremiah 36:1-8
Hebrews 1:1, 2; Ephesians 3:1-5

Why is there such a thing as the Bible in the first place?
Why is it here? What is its purpose?

To answer these queries we must deal with some even
more basic questions: Why is there such a thing as the
universe, including this earth? Why does man himself
exist? Why are we here? What is our purpose?

To couch the question in Biblical terms, why did God
create man? The answer is that He desired to make a
creature in His own image who could love Him and serve
Him, with whom He could have personal fellowship
forever. The earth itself was to be the stage for this inti-
mate communion.

Genesis 3:8 gives us a clue concerning this purpose.
Following Adam and Eve's initial sin, "they heard the
sound of the Lord God walking in the garden in the cool
of the day." But because they were now stricken with
guilt, they "hid themselves from the presence of the Lord
God." The implication is that God had joined them in this
manner before, since they recognized the signs of His
presence. It is also implied that they had welcomed His

visits, their hiding now being motivated by their own sin-wrought shame.

It is difficult for us to imagine the delight that must have been shared by Creator and creature alike in these moments of face-to-face communion. This was not Adam and Eve's sole activity, since they had been given definite tasks to perform and other things on which to concentrate (Genesis 1:28, 2:15). But surely this was the climactic event of the day, when God came to them personally, and they shared their lives with Him in holy innocence and joy.

It is difficult to imagine a more immediate form of revelation than the manner in which God showed himself to Adam and Eve in the garden. We are not to think that God was appearing to them in His pure spiritual essence (Exodus 33:20). It was, however, the most direct of "theophanies" or divine appearances: God himself was present, perhaps in human form, walking and talking with those made in His own spiritual image. There was no need for a Bible then.

The entrance of sin, however, ended the intimacy. A whole new set of circumstances prevailed. Sin broke the fellowship between God and man, introduced guilt and corruption into the world, and set mankind on the road to eternal death and separation from God. Sadly but necessarily, God withdrew His direct, personal presence from among His creatures. See Isaiah 59:1, 2.

But God had foreseen this course of events, and was prepared to set into motion a plan that would ultimately restore the fellowship. Included in this plan was the writing of the Bible.

The Need for Revelation

The first and basic need created by sin was the need for *redemption.* Man must be redeemed from the state and consequences of his sin. He must be rescued and restored. Though the plan of redemption was conceived in the mind of God before creation (Matthew 25:34; 1 Peter 1:18-20), it could be accomplished only within the framework of history itself.

God's plan included a long series of historical events, beginning with the call of Abraham to found the nation that would be the context of all future redemptive events. These included the development of Israel within the womb of Egypt, the labor pains of the Exodus and wilderness wanderings, and the birth of the nation in the land of Canaan. For the next millennium, working through judges, kings, and prophets, God continued to set the stage for the final and decisive act in the drama of redemption: the life, death, and resurrection of the incarnate Christ.

In addition to this need for redemption was the secondary but vital need for *revelation.* Although God was no longer personally present upon the earth, it was still necessary for Him to communicate in some way with His people. The mighty redemptive acts of God (for example, those related to the exodus from Egypt, or the resurrection of Jesus) revealed His power and nature to some degree, but their purpose was redemption, not revelation. Something was needed in addition to the events themselves.

Why is there a need for revelation? In a very general sense we may say that God simply wants to keep the lines of communication open between himself and His people. He wants to let us know that He still loves us in spite of our sin, that He is doing something to solve the problem, and that salvation is indeed available to us if we will receive it.

Also, generally speaking, revelation is necessary in order that God may keep before us the truth about himself and ourselves. It is also needed to show us the nature of a godly life (2 Timothy 3:16, 17).

Speaking more specifically, though, we should say that revelation is needed in order to *explain* the redemption

16

that God has worked out in history. Redemption might indeed be accomplished without revelation, but how then would we understand what it is all about? How would we know how to receive it for ourselves and participate in its benefits? For instance, can we imagine Jesus coming as the incarnate son of God, dying for our sins, departing from the tomb, and returning to the Father without a word of explanation?

It is obvious that without a revealed explanation of the redemptive events, the whole enterprise would be in vain. It would remain a mystery forever hidden in God (see Ephesians 3:1-11). With revelation, however, we can know what God has done to save us, and we can know how to receive it (1 Corinthians 15:1-4; 2 Timothy 3:15).

The Need for *Word* Revelation

It is necessary also that this revelation be given to us in the form of words. Of course, some revelation is possible without words, such as the knowledge of God that comes to us through nature (Psalm 19:1-6; Romans 1:18-21). Because of our sin, though, we are inclined to ignore it or distort it (Romans 1:21-32). Besides, this general revelation (as it is called) does not tell us about redemption. Indeed, it could not do so, since redemption can be understood only through the communication of information, that is, only through *word* revelation.

Words are the most natural form of communication for intelligent beings, especially when one is not visible to the other. Through the use of words, ideas, and concepts are transferred from one mind to another.

This is exactly what is required when something has to be *explained,* especially something as profound as the plan of salvation. Signs, gestures, symbolic acts (even the "mighty acts of God," the redemptive acts themselves) do not explain. Indeed they are the very things that *need* explaining, and explanation is a function performed through *words.*

What happens when there is activity without explanation? Either we remain ignorant of its meaning, or we form our own subjective opinions as to what it is all about. The more intense and complex the activity, the more we are at the mercy of our own subjectivity.

Edith Schaeffer illustrates this perfectly through an incident involving an in-flight showing of the movie *Jaws*. She had declined the earphones that would provide the movie's sound, hoping to do some paper work. Occasionally, however, squeals from other passengers caused her to glance at the screen, where she saw—without the accompanying words—such scenes as people running on the beach, someone thrashing in the water, and someone in a hospital. She comments, "What a garbled account I would give of the film if I depended on the impressions my eyes were giving me, without the words!" Without "verbalized explanation," she says, we often misinterpret what we see and arrive at false conclusions.

Two things are clear: we need a verbal communication from God; and we are, after all, intelligent creatures accustomed to using language. In view of these two facts, it is rather inconceivable that God would choose *not* to use words or speech in revealing himself, His will, and the nature of His salvation.

The truth is that *God has spoken* (Hebrews 1:1-3). This is the overwhelming testimony of Scripture. The expression "Thus saith the Lord" or its equivalent occurs nearly two thousand times in the Old Testament alone. "The word of the Lord" came through the prophets (see 1 Kings 16:1; Hosea 1:1). God told Jeremiah, "Behold, I have put my words in your mouth" (Jeremiah 1:9). Scripture is called the "oracles of God" (Romans 3:2). Jesus declares that we must live by "every word that proceeds out of the mouth of God" (Matthew 4:4). Such references and examples could be greatly multiplied.

Why is it important to stress this point? Because one of the most common views of revelation today is that God reveals himself through His "mighty acts," but *never* through words or propositions. Many liberal churchmen hold this view. Their idea is not simply that God does not speak, but that He *cannot* speak in our language.

This view is based not on Scripture or evidence of any kind, but only on an unprovable presupposition about the nature of God and His relationship to history. It is assumed that the difference between God and man is so vast that our relative, culture-bound language cannot contain or express divine concepts. The idea is that God is to man what man is to mice or insects. Even Einstein could not explain the theory of relativity to ants. Neither can God reduce His thoughts to human language, according to the speculations of these churchmen.

This objection to word revelation is false. At least two lines of reasoning make this plain.

First, it is true that God is different from man. But it is this very difference that enables God to speak to us despite our differences. We cannot discuss philosophical concepts with insects because we are finite, limited. But God is *God,* the infinite, the almighty, the all-knowing God. Let us not try to impose our limitations upon Him.

Second, word revelation is proper and effective because we are made in God's image (Genesis 1:26, 27) and are thus by nature adapted to communicating with Him. To use an analogy, our receiver is already tuned in to God's wavelength. He made us for the very purpose of communing and communicating with Him.

Thus God is able to speak to us, revealing the things we need to know about our redemption; and we who are in His image are able to understand His words.

The Need for *Written* Revelation

God's plan of redemption included one further requirement with regard to revelation; it must be in *written* form. Of course, not every word of revelation has been put into writing, but much of it has. God himself set the pattern by writing the Ten Commandments on tablets of stone with His own "finger" (Exodus 31:18), even after He had spoken them audibly (Deuteronomy 5:22). Moses wrote down the rest of the law at God's command (Exodus 24:4; 34:27).

When God sent the prophets, He sent them not only to preach but also to write. He said to Jeremiah, "Write all the words which I have spoken to you in a book" (Jeremiah 30:2; see 36:2). With regard to his Gospel, Luke was inspired by the Spirit to say, "It seemed fitting for me . . . to write it out for you" (Luke 1:3). When the Lord was preparing John to receive His Revelation, He commanded him, "Write in a book what you see" (Revelation 1:11, 19).

Why is it fitting and necessary for revelation to be written? There are several reasons. First, this puts it in *permanent* form so that it is available to future generations as well as to the people who immediately receive it. The redemptive acts are one-time events; they must be recorded and explained for all times. Revelation itself, since it is given to particular persons in specific historical circumstances, must be put into a form that is permanently available. The written Old Testament still continues, by God's design, to benefit Christians (Romans 4:22-25; 1 Corinthians 10:11); and the gospel of Jesus Christ, being preserved in written form, is still bringing people to faith and eternal life (John 20:30, 31).

A second reason for preserving the revelation in writing is that it thereby becomes an *objective* standard, accessible to all in the same form and the same way. The written revelation invalidates all appeals to subjective experience: inner voices, personal "revelations," intuitive opinions, visions, and feelings. All such phenomena are highly individualized and inherently ambiguous. The only sure source of truth is the objective word of Scripture. This is confirmed by the way Christ and the New Testament writers constantly appeal to the words of the

Old Testament: "It is written . . . it is written . . . it is written." (For example, see Matthew 4:10; Romans 1:17).

Still another reason why God's revelation is put into written form is that this gives it a certain *finality* that befits its absolute authority. When a law or a judgment or a prophecy is written, that makes it final and firm and solid. It should be done, it shall be done, it *must* be done. That God wrote the Ten Commandments in stone symbolizes this immutability. See also Deuteronomy 27:2, 3, 8; Joshua 8:32. He ordered His judgments to be written as an everlasting testimony and warning of His justice (Exodus 17:14; Isaiah 30:8). Once written, His word must not be changed (Revelation 22:18, 19). It is decisive and absolute, down to the smallest letter and stroke (Matthew 5:17, 18).

We must not forget that God's primary purpose is redemption; He is working to restore us to personal fellowship with himself. A necessary part of His redemptive plan, though, is word revelation made available in written form. This has been provided. It is the Bible. "Seek ye out of the book of the Lord, and read" (Isaiah 34:16, King James Version).

3

The Inspiration of Scripture

1 Peter 1:10-12; 2 Peter 1:19-21
2 Timothy 3:14-17
John 14:26; 16:12-15

The Bible is God's *communication* to man. Communication is basically concerned with ideas. It is the transfer of an idea or concept from one person's mind to another person's mind. The Bible thus is God's way of transferring certain concepts from His mind to ours.

Communication is usually accomplished by means of symbols such as pictures, gestures, or words. Since words have the greatest versatility and precision, most communication takes this form. This includes the Bible.

Good communication is not easy. If one has an idea he wants to communicate to someone else, he must be careful to choose just the right words, the ones that most precisely represent the idea in his mind. These must also be words that the intended hearer can understand, words that mean the same thing to him as to the speaker. Of course, this is no problem for an all-wise God.

There is one other factor, however, that may considerably complicate the process of communication. What if the speaker desires to pass his message along by means of a third party? How can he be sure the spokesman will remember and present the message in its original form? This problem is well illustrated by the party game called "Gossip." With the players seated in a circle, one person whispers a brief statement to the person next to him, who then whispers it to his neighbor as he heard it, and so on. The last person to hear the statement speaks it aloud, and it invariably differs wildly from the original version. It has become hopelessly garbled in the process of transmission.

Since God has chosen to communicate with us through spokesmen or prophets, He has had to face this problem. When God reveals His message to the prophet, He knows the proper words are being used. But how can He be sure the prophet will pass the message along just as he received it? Here is where inspiration enters the picture. *Inspiration* is the term used to refer to the special supernatural supervision exercised by God over His messengers to make sure they communicate His message accurately. The men who wrote the Bible were thus inspired or supervised; therefore we can rest assured that it is what God intended the writers to say. This is why inspiration is all-important. Because of it, we know when we are reading the Bible that we are reading the *Word of God*.

The Fact of Inspiration

The Bible clearly teaches that it is inspired. Even though the word *inspiration* itself seldom appears, the fact that God himself is speaking through the Biblical writers is often affirmed.

Matthew 1:22 establishes this familiar pattern. Referring to the prophecy in Isaiah 7:14, it says that the words were actually spoken *by the Lord,* but spoken *through* the prophet as the Lord's instrument. See also Matthew 2:15; Hebrews 4:7. Luke 1:70 says that the Lord God "spoke by the mouth of His holy prophets from of old." See also Acts 3:18; 4:25.

23

The Holy Spirit appears to play the major role in the production of Scripture through the prophets and apostles. Nehemiah 9:30 uses the same formula appearing later in the New Testament: "By Thy Spirit through Thy prophets." David gives the Spirit credit for the message he speaks: "The Spirit of the Lord spoke by me, and His word was on my tongue" (2 Samuel 23:2). The New Testament confirms this: "The Holy Spirit foretold by the mouth of David" the fate of Judas (Acts 1:16).

Paul says, "The Holy Spirit rightly spoke through Isaiah the prophet" about the Jews' hardness of heart (Acts 28:25). Both David and John were "in the Spirit" when they wrote (Matthew 22:43; Revelation 1:10). Peter says that it was "the Spirit of Christ" working within the prophets who was responsible for the many predictions about Jesus (1 Peter 1:10, 11).

The most striking reference to the Holy Spirit's role in inspiration is 2 Peter 1:20, 21, which says, "But know this first of all, that no prophecy of Scripture is a matter of one's own interpretation, for no prophecy was ever made by an act of human will, but men moved by the Holy Spirit spoke from God." That is to say, the prophets were not just giving their own interpretations of God's works. The "prophetic word" (verse 19) was not just the result of human investigation; it was not the product of the writers' own thinking. Instead, as they spoke, they were being "carried along" by the Spirit. This is the literal meaning of "moved" in verse 21.

We must remember, too, that Jesus promised the apostles that the Spirit would guide them in their presentation of the truth (John 14:26; 16:12-15). Thus Peter says that they preached the gospel "by the Holy Spirit sent from heaven" (1 Peter 1:12; see Ephesians 3:5). Paul knew that the Spirit was guiding him in his writing (1 Corinthians 7:40; 1 Timothy 4:1).

The classic affirmation of the inspiration of the Bible is 2 Timothy 3:16: "All Scripture is inspired by God." The

English words "inspired by God" are the translation of a single Greek word, *theopneustos,* which literally means "breathed out by God," or "God-breathed." The divine origin of the written word could not be more clearly attested.

The Scope of Inspiration

Now that the fact of inspiration has been noted, several other questions must be raised. One has to do with the *scope* of inspiration. Exactly what is inspired? We answer first that God's *messengers* were inspired. Supernatural power was exerted upon the men themselves. Second Peter 1:21 says the prophets were borne along by the Holy Spirit. In this sense, inspiration was that supernatural influence upon selected men which enabled them to communicate God's message exactly as *He* wanted it done.

But we must go further. Inspiration applies not only to messengers. Their *message* itself is inspired; it is Scripture that is God-breathed (2 Timothy 3:16). In this sense, inspiration is a quality imparted to the writing as a result of the influence upon the writer. (This is important to note, because some Bible critics are willing to say that the *writers* were inspired, but that this did not make their *writing* special. To say this, though, one must deny Scripture.)

One limitation should be noted. Inspiration applies only to the original manuscripts of the books of the Bible, the ones that came directly from the hands of the human authors themselves. These are called the "autographs."

Another important point in relation to the scope of inspiration is that the *whole* Bible is inspired. Every part of it was produced under divine guidance of the Holy Spirit. Thus inspiration is "plenary" or entire.

This means the New Testament as well as the Old Testament is inspired. Paul says that *all* Scripture is God-breathed (2 Timothy 3:16). The word *Scripture* is not limited to the Old Testament. In 1 Timothy 5:18 Paul gives two quotations. One is from Deuteronomy 25:4; the other is from Matthew 10:10 (and Luke 10:7). Both, he says, are *Scripture*. Peter writes about Paul's letters and *the rest* of the Scriptures (2 Peter 3:15, 16), thus putting Paul's writing into the category of Scripture. The prophets and the apostles are equally thought of as spokesmen for the Lord (1 Peter 1:10-12; 2 Peter 3:2).

To say that the whole Bible is inspired also means that every *kind* of Biblical writing bears the quality of inspiration. This applies to the historical sections as well as the doctrinal and didactic. Some try to make a distinction here and limit the divine influence only to the latter. There is no objective basis for this limitation, however. Jesus rebuked those who did not believe in *all* the prophets had spoken (Luke 24:25). He himself quoted with equal ease and confidence from both the historical and the theological content of the Old Testament. (See chapter 1 above.) Paul testified that he believed *everything* written in the law and the prophets (Acts 24:14).

One final point with regard to the scope of inspiration is that the divine influence extended not only to the *thoughts* being conveyed but to the very *words* by which they were conveyed. Without this inclusion, the whole purpose of inspiration is defeated, since the key to accurate communication of ideas is the choice of proper and precise words. As Clark Pinnock has said, "If inspiration had nothing to do with words, it would be irrelevant."

Paul illustrates the importance of the individual words of Scripture when he stresses the singular form of the word "seed" in Genesis 22:18 (Galatians 3:16). Jesus himself says that *every word* is important (Matthew 4:4), and that even the letters and parts of letters can be considered authoritative (Matthew 5:18). Even if the latter statement is hyperbolic (exaggerated for emphasis), it serves to accent the fact that God's concern for the accuracy of Scripture is all-inclusive.

The Manner of Inspiration

A question that usually arises in this context is the *manner* of inspiration: exactly how did the Holy Spirit influence the authors of Scripture? The Bible gives very little information on this point. We must remember that God's purpose in inspiration was to make sure that His spokesmen transmitted the exact message that He desired. Because the communication involved different kinds of messages, all the way from totally new revealed material to personally-witnessed historical data, the divine activity was no doubt more intense at some times than at others.

With regard to generally-available historical material or personal feelings and experiences, the Spirit needed to exercise only a general kind of supervision. For instance, Luke says that he did a great deal of historical research before writing his Gospel (Luke 1:1-4). The Spirit needed only to make sure that he uncovered all the facts needed for this particular Gospel and that he communicated them accurately. The same applies to the book of Acts, except that Luke was actually present at many of the events he describes in that book. See a long passage beginning at Acts 20:5. In such cases, the Spirit would simply quicken his memory and guarantee its accuracy.

In other situations, though, a more active participation by the Holy Spirit was needed. For instance, the prophets often were enabled to utter predictions that they did not understand (1 Peter 1:10, 11). As God told Moses, "I . . . will be with your mouth, and teach you what you are to say" (Exodus 4:12; see Matthew 10:19, 20).

Bible critics often accuse Bible-believers of teaching that Scripture is the product of "mechanical dictation," and that the writers were just machines that the Holy Spirit used like tape-recorders. The critics ridicule such a view and distort the concept of inspiration.

Such an approach is not only erroneous; it is highly unfair and dishonest. No responsible Bible-believer holds to such a "dictation theory" of inspiration. Even in cases where the Biblical authors were most dependent on the Spirit, they were not in a passive, unconscious state. Pagan religions, ancient and modern, abound with the religious oracle or shaman who speaks for the "deity" while in a trance or state of possession. There is no hint of this kind of thing involving the Biblical writers, however. They were conscious of their activity; their full natural personality was operative; they spoke and wrote in their own vocabulary and literary style.

J. W. McGarvey makes this point:

> It would be nearer the truth to compare the whole work of the Spirit to that of driving a well trained horse. You draw the lines to the right or the left as you see that the horse needs guidance; you check him when he would go too fast, and urge him forward when he would go too slow; but he usually keeps the road and maintains the desired gait and speed of his own accord; still your hand is ever on the lines, and its pressure on the bit is constantly felt, so that you are controlling the horse's movements when he is going most completely at his own will. Indeed, the horse is all the time going very much at his own will, and yet he is never without the control of the driver.

We should not be concerned if we cannot describe in detail the manner of inspiration. After all, the most important aspect of it is not the nature of the *process,* but the nature of the *product.* Whatever the form of supervision used by the Spirit, we are assured that it produced the message that God desired. That is what matters.

The Result of Inspiration

What is the result of inspiration? What kind of book is the inspired Bible? It is *God's own Word*. God was in full control of its production; what was written down was what He wanted to be written; thus it is fully proper to call it the Word of God.

Paul knew the difference between the mere word of man and the word of God. He said to the Thessalonians, "And for this reason we also constantly thank God that when you received from us the word of God's message, you accepted it not as the word of men, but for what it really is, the word of God" (1 Thessalonians 2:13). Thus Paul knew his own message to be the word of God, just as he knew the Old Testament to be the "oracles" or words of God (Romans 3:2). Jeremiah knew his writing to be the words of God (Jeremiah 36:2). As we have seen, Jesus referred to the Old Testament as the word of God (Matthew 15:6).

Some object to calling the Bible the Word of God, saying that only Jesus rightly deserves this title. Certainly Jesus is called the Word of God (John 1:1; Revelation 19:13). But in the New Testament itself, the expression "word of God" is used far more often for the spoken or written message than for Jesus. For some examples see Acts 4:31; 6:2, 7; 8:14; 11:1; 13:5, 7, 44, 46; 17:13; 18:11.

To refer to the Bible as the Word of God does not take away from Jesus' glory as the living, incarnate Word. Likewise to call Jesus the Word of God does not make the Bible only a second-rate word. They are both truly and really the Word of God, but in different senses. Scripture is the Word of God in the sense that its words have their origin in the very mind of God. As J. I. Packer says, "When we hear or read Scripture, that which impinges on our mind (whether we realize it or not) is the speech of God himself."

One further point must be made. Since the Bible is God-breathed and thus is the very Word of God, how can we resist the conclusion that it is absolutely accurate, true, and without error? How can we deny the inerrancy of Scripture? This is the subject of the next chapter.

4

The Inerrancy of the Bible

John 10:30-39; 17:14-19; 20:30, 31

One of the most crucial and widely-discussed issues facing the church today is the nature of the Bible. At the heart of the discussion is the question of inerrancy. Is the Bible inerrant in everything it asserts? In light of what we have seen thus far in this study, the answer must be *yes*. This is the only view that is consistent with Biblical teaching and Christian commitment.

Inerrancy: the Biblical Teaching

What does the word *inerrant* mean? It means "without error, mistake, contradiction, or falsehood." It means "true, reliable, trustworthy, accurate, infallible." To say that the Bible is inerrant means that it is absolutely true and trustworthy in everything it asserts; it is totally without error.

Inerrancy is not just a theory about the Bible or a philosophical concept alien to the Bible, as some critics say. The doctrine of Biblical inerrancy is firmly rooted in the teaching of Scripture itself, where it is both implied and asserted.

The argument for inerrancy is more than a mere inference. It is actually a syllogism, which is a form of argument in which the conclusion is necessarily true if the two premises are true, as in the following classic example: "All men are mortal (major premise); Socrates is a man (minor premise); therefore Socrates is mortal (necessary conclusion)."

In the argument for inerrancy, the major premise is "Every word of God is true (inerrant)." This may rightly be inferred from the very nature of God, since God cannot lie (Titus 1:2). But it is also specifically affirmed. Jesus said to the Father, "Thy word is truth" (John 17:17). His word is called "the word of truth" (2 Corinthians 6:7; Colossians 1:5; 2 Timothy 2:15; James 1:18).

The minor premise of the argument is "The Bible is God's Word." This premise is also established both by inference and by direct assertion. It is the proper and necessary inference from the fact of inspiration. All Scripture is God-breathed (2 Timothy 3:16), which means that God himself is its origin and source. It is *His* Word, the Word of *God.* In addition to inference, though, is the direct assertion. Scripture is *called* "the word of God" in Matthew 15:6 (see Mark 7:13), Romans 9:6, and Psalm 119:105. Even more emphatically, Scripture is called "the oracles of God" (that is, the words God *said)* in Romans 3:2, where the term refers to the whole Old Testament, and in Hebrews 5:12, where it includes the New Testament revelation as well.

Since both the major and minor premises are true, the conclusion follows by logical necessity. Every word of God is true (inerrant); the Bible is God's Word; therefore the Bible is inerrant. This can be denied only by denying one or both of the premises. Even if one rejects this solid argument, there is still another point that must be faced. That the Bible is inerrant is not just the necessary conclusion of a sound syllogism; *it is also directly taught in the Word of God.* Jesus specifically declared that "Scripture cannot be broken" (John 10:35). Whatever is written in Scripture is absolute truth; Scripture is the infallible authority. This statement by Jesus is the solid foundation on which the doctrine of Biblical inerrancy rests.

The Biblical evidence for inerrancy can be summed up as follows:

A. Major Premise: "Every word of God is true (inerrant)."
   1. Inference from God's nature
   2. Direct assertion of Scripture
B. Minor Premise: "The Bible is God's Word."
   1. Inference from the fact of inspiration
   2. Direct assertion of Scripture
C. Conclusion: "The Bible is true (inerrant)."
   1. Logical necessity from A and B
   2. Direct assertion of Scripture

We should not be surprised at this conclusion, since the very purpose of inspiration is to assure the accuracy of the communication God gives to man through His spokesmen. This is the very goal and rationale of inspiration; this is why God inspired the writers in the first place.

Why is the inerrancy of the Scripture such a crucial point? If the Bible were no more important than any other book, then it would not really matter. The need for accuracy in any writing is directly related to the importance of the writing. Vacation postcards could contain errors of fact, and little would depend on it. If a road map is wrong it may be inconvenient but not fatal. On the other hand, mistakes in military communications and command decisions could be very costly in terms of lives and freedom.

But the most important message of all is the one God is communicating to us through Scripture. It is a matter of life and death, indeed, *eternal* life or *eternal* death. These things "have been written that you may believe that Jesus is the Christ, the Son of God; and that believing you may have life in His name" (John 20:31). Here is a message of such importance that God has not trusted it to fallible memories and understandings. He has supervised its communication so that it reaches us without error.

Inerrancy: Contemporary Denials

Despite the strong Biblical teaching on inerrancy, it has many enemies, even among those who have a general trust in the Bible's reliability. Harold Lindsell's book, *The Battle for the Bible,* has called attention to this fact for conservative Protestantism in general. Even among people devoted to the restoration of New Testament Christianity, increasing numbers seem to doubt or deny that the Bible is without error.

As might be expected, the denial is plainer among the more liberal groups. Ralph Wilburn is a theologian for the Disciples of Christ. In *The Reconstruction of Theology* he says that Disciples now view Scripture as "a historical human witness" rather than as an infallible book.

Also in the churches of Christ (usually regarded as very conservative) there are voices speaking out against inerrancy. An example is Leroy Garrett's article, "The Inspiration of the Scriptures" in *Restoration Review* of October, 1975. While denying any "substantial error" or "material mistakes," Mr. Garrett does allow that the Bible has errors.

Many Christians and many congregations are in the group that J. D. Murch calls "centrist." They seek to avoid both the liberalism of the Disciples associated with Ralph Wilburn, and the extremes of the churches associated with Leroy Garrett. Here also, several writers have belittled the doctrine of inerrancy, calling it an irrelevant or insignificant theory. For example, H. E. Johnson writes to the editor of *Christian Standard* that the doctrine of inerrancy is not taught in Scripture and should be abandoned.

Inerrancy: Limited or Unlimited?

Many who think they find errors in the Bible are not willing to abandon inerrancy completely, however. They prefer to accept what is called "limited inerrancy" or "partial inerrancy." Daniel Fuller is a well-known representative of this view. He explains it in an article called "The Nature of Biblical Inerrancy," in the *Journal of the American Scientific Affiliation* (June 1972). Here he says that inerrancy applies only to the things that fall within the intention of the authors, which was "to report the happenings and meaning of the redemptive acts of God in history so that men might be made wise unto salvation" (p. 47). These are *revealed* truths, he says; they are verbally inspired and inerrant.

However, says Fuller, the Bible contains many incidental statements about "non-revelational matters" such as geology, botany, and geography. While the Holy Spirit enabled the writers to make the best use of such material, He was not concerned with inerrancy in this area, in Fuller's opinion.

This same kind of "partial inerrancy" is being advocated by many others. William Robinson defends a concept of "infallibility with limits" in *The Biblical Doctrine of the Church*. Leroy Garrett says he accepts inerrancy "in those things essential to the main purpose of scripture." H. E. Johnson accepts the idea of limited inerrancy, saying that "the infallibility of the Bible pertains only to the Gospel of Jesus Christ."

Some who feel uncomfortable with the term *inerrancy* suggest that we use other terms, such as *reliability* and *trustworthiness*. One writer says he accepts the Bible as "reliable, trustworthy, and true," but does not think the doctrine of inerrancy is helpful or relevant. This is a false distinction between terms. Anything that is reliable, trustworthy, and true is *inerrant*. At whatever point or to whatever degree it is errant, it is unreliable or untrustworthy. When one says the Bible is trustworthy and true, except in those places where errors occur, he is really asserting partial or limited inerrancy.

Whatever its form, the doctrine of partial inerrancy is unacceptable. This is true for three reasons.

First, there is absolutely no Biblical basis for a distinction between that which is inspired and inerrant and that which is uninspired and liable to error. It *is* proper to distinguish between that which is revealed and that which is not revealed. In the latter category are historical data uncovered by research or known by personal experience. But it is false to say that such non-revelational matters were not *inspired* and therefore may have errors. Jesus specifically promised that the Spirit would guard the apostolic memories (John 14:26). When they wrote, the apostles were inspired to recall and properly record what God wanted them to record.

The scope of Biblical inerrancy is equal to the scope of inspiration. (See chapter 3.) Although it pertains only to the autographs or original manuscripts, it applies to *every part* of them, history as well as doctrine, words as well as ideas. When Jesus said we should believe "all that the prophets have spoken" (Luke 24:25), and when Paul said he believed "everything" in the law and prophets (Acts 24:14) no exceptions were given.

Second, if we think the Bible is not all true, we can never be sure at what points it is true and at what points it is false. The arbitrary distinction between revelational and non-revelational matters is especially disconcerting. The idea is that non-revelational matters include things we can test and check by historical or scientific investigation; these may prove to be either true or false. But the revelational matters, which by their very nature cannot be tested, are assumed to be inerrant!

This is a very unsettling procedure. If a writing proves to contain errors in those areas that can be checked, why should we assume that the rest of it is free from errors? The tendency, in fact, would be the very opposite.

The final reason why partial inerrancy is unacceptable is that it is impossible to defend. Those who limit inerrancy usually accept it in matters of "faith and practice" or the revelational and doctrinal portions of Scripture. But we must remember that inerrancy is itself a Biblical doctrine: *The Bible teaches its own inerrancy.* If error is found in *any* part of Scripture, then this teaching is the biggest error of all—and it is in the area of doctrine, the very part that is supposed to be free from error! If we cannot trust the Bible's doctrine of Scripture, how can we trust *any* of its doctrine?

The alternatives seem to be total inerrancy or no inerrancy. Either the Bible is inerrant in everything it asserts, or there is no guarantee of inerrancy in anything it says. The only position consistent with Biblical teaching is that the Bible is totally without error.

5

Objections to Inerrancy

Psalm 19:7-11; Matthew 5:17, 18; 22:23-33
Acts 24:14

The Bible is inerrant, according to its own teaching. This is the belief of countless thoughtful, Bible-believing people. Many others would like to accept it, but find themselves disturbed by the objections that are constantly being raised against it.

In this chapter we will attempt to answer some of the most common of these objections. Our goal is to show that our confidence in Scripture is not misplaced.

"Inerrancy Is a New Concept"

One objection that occurs regularly, despite a wealth of available data to the contrary, is that inerrancy is a new view. It is sometimes linked with early twentieth-century fundamentalism, the implication being that only someone with a "fundamentalist mentality" would believe it. More often it is traced to some aspect of seventeenth century Protestant orthodoxy. The following statement is typical: "The concept of Biblical inerrancy is an old one in Protestantism, finding its first expression in the Canons of the Synod of Dort (1618-19)."

Inerrancy is *not* a new view, and it was not new in 1618. In fact, it was the continuous mainstream view of the church from the first century, through the Reformation, down to the rise of rationalism and negative criticism in the eighteenth century. This book could be filled with quotations to this effect, but space limits us to only a few examples.

Clement of Rome, writing perhaps as early as A.D. 95, said, "You have studied the Holy Scriptures, which are true and inspired by the Holy Spirit. You know nothing contrary to justice or truth has been written in them." Irenaeus in the late second century said that "the Scriptures are indeed perfect, since they were spoken by the Word of God and His Spirit." Augustine in the early fifth century wrote, "For I confess . . . that I have learned to yield this respect and honour only to the canonical books of Scripture: of these alone do I most firmly believe that the authors were completely free from error."

Martin Luther praised this statement, saying that "St. Augustine, in a letter to St. Jerome, has put down a fine axiom—that only Holy Scripture is to be considered inerrant." Luther voiced this opinion many times. "For the Word of God is perfect; . . . it is truth itself. There is no falsehood in it." "Scripture . . . has never erred." "God's Word cannot err." So said Luther.

John Calvin likewise referred to Scripture as the "sure and infallible record," the "unerring standard," the "certain and unerring rule," the "unerring light," and the "infallible word of God." He said it is "free from every stain or defect."

The references from Luther and Calvin are especially important because many people now have the misconception that neither of those leaders believed the Bible to be inerrant. For example, J. D. Smart has said, "It is at once significant that for Luther and Calvin verbal inspiration did not involve inerrancy." This is definitely an errant reading of the reformers.

38

A variation of this desperate desire to have one's heroes agree with him is seen in some who are involved in the present movement to restore New Testament Christianity. Since Alexander Campbell was a leader of that movement, some try to show that he did not believe in inerrancy. The attempt is in vain, however.

Campbell accepted the distinction between the revealed truth and the non-revealed facts of Scripture, as he explained in his debate with Robert Owen. Revelation, he said, is "Divine communication concerning spiritual and eternal things." But in addition, "there are a thousand historic facts narrated in the Bible." These include "topographical and historic facts and incidents; . . . narratives, geographical and biographical notices, etc." Campbell distinguished such "ordinary information" from "the divine communications." Nevertheless, he declared that *both* are inspired and therefore inerrant:

> Moreover, the persons who are employed to make these communications are so supernaturally guided as to make them infallible witnesses in all the facts they attest, as well as all the communications concerning supernatural things.

In this statement, "all the facts they attest" refers to the historic, non-revealed data of Scripture.

Exactly the same point was made in an article in the 1846 *Millennial Harbinger.* Here Campbell wrote both of the inspiration of revealed truth and of the "supernatural aid afforded the saints who wrote the historical parts of the sacred scriptures." He said there was given to them "such a superintendency of the Spirit of wisdom and knowledge as excluded the possibility of mistake in the matters of fact which they recorded." Thus he recognized "inspiration in its primary and secondary import," which "precluded the selection of incorrect or unsuitable words and sentences."

Clearly, then, the idea of an inerrant Bible is not a "new view" in our century. Neither was it a "new view" when the Synod of Dort recognized it in 1618 or 1619. It is the view held by Christians in all the centuries since Christianity began.

"Inerrancy Ignores the Human Side of Scripture"

Another common objection to inerrancy is that it ignores the fact that the Bible is the product of human authors. Since divine revelation has been given through "earthen vessels," as one critic asserts, it "consequently has the mark of human imperfections." To deny the presence of errors is likened to Docetism, which denied the humanity of Christ. As one writer puts it, "The fact is that Scripture, though God-breathed, comes to us in the form of fallible human language from a fallible human witness."

Certainly the Bible has a human side. Its human authors were fragile, weak, and limited; they were by nature liable to error, deception, sin, imperfection. The monstrous fallacy of this objection to inerrancy, however, is the confusion of *possibility* with *necessity.* It assumes that whatever is by nature human must *necessarily* err, that humanness *requires* imperfection, either moral (sin) or intellectual (error).

This is a patently false assumption. Humanness does not *ipso facto* imply imperfection. Adam and Eve, when first created, were finite but unflawed; and their sin was not inevitable. Jesus himself had a truly human nature, but this involved Him in neither sin nor error.

We can grant the *possibility* of error on the part of fallible men without assuming its *necessity.* In fact, the *possibility* of error is the very reason for inspiration. If errors were not possible, inspiration would not have been needed. But if errors were inevitable, then inspiration would have been futile. The very purpose of the

Spirit's supervision was to keep men who *could* err from doing so.

One other point should be noted. The same "fallible" men who recorded the history also wrote the revealed message of salvation. Thus it is inconsistent to urge that humanness implies fallibility and to hold a theory of limited inerrancy at the same time. If humanness must taint the history, in spite of inspiration, then it must taint the doctrine, too. But likewise, if the Holy Spirit can protect the doctrine from corruption in spite of the humanness of the authors, He can protect the history, too.

"Inerrancy Is Irrelevant, Since the Autographs Were Not Preserved"

Another common objection to inerrancy is based on the fact that the only documents that were truly inerrant—the original manuscripts or autographs—are no longer in existence. In the process of making countless copies of the Biblical books, the scribes made many errors. Thus, as one critic says, the only texts we have available today are flawed. To be sure, none of the errors is serious regarding either history or doctrine. They are all minor mistakes. Still, they exist in all the Bibles we use, and the critic says this "raises a question concerning the relevance of the contention that once there was an inerrant original."

It is true that the autographs have disappeared. (This is probably by God's design, since they probably would have been idolized had they remained in existence.) But this does not mean that we must remain uncertain about what they said. So many *copies* were made that by comparing them we can determine what was in the originals. Apart from trivial variations such as those in spelling and word order, it is estimated that we can be sure of ninety-nine and nine-tenths percent of the original New Testament text, and the remaining one tenth of one percent contains nothing crucial.

Thus the reconstructed text is nearly perfect. When we read it, for all practical purposes we *are* reading what was in the originals.

If we can get along with our flawed copies, then why does it matter so much whether the originals were inerrant or not? If there are errors in the Bibles we use, what difference does it make whether there were errors in the original or not?

Let us consider the alternatives. In the Book you depend on to guide you to eternal life, would you rather have a nearly-perfect copy of an original with no mistakes in it, or a nearly-perfect copy of an original with mistakes? Can anyone really say the difference is irrelevant? The faultless character of the original gives value to the copies, even if the copies are not faultless.

Suppose you must take a long trip across a treacherous desert. It is a dangerous trip, but by following the map and directions carefully, you can make it. The map and directions were prepared by a man who had crossed the desert many times and knew it practically by heart. The only difficulty is that the original manuscript of his directions has been lost. It was copied so many times, though, that a reliable reconstruction has been made.

While you are pondering whether to trust this "mere copy," another man standing nearby says to you, "Look, I know this desert. I crossed it once about twenty years ago. Let me draw you a map and write out the directions for you myself."

If this were your choice, you would not hesitate to choose the former.

The same is true regarding the Bible: nearly-perfect copies of inerrant originals are infinitely preferable to even perfect copies of errant originals. *The nature and character of the originals determine the worth of the copies.*

Here is another important point. Even though there are variations in our existing copies that leave us uncertain about a few places in the text, *we know where those places are.* By an objective procedure (textual criticism), the uncertain areas are identified. Thus we know where there is no doubt about the original text, and we know we can trust what it says *because it is the inerrant word of God.* But even if we had perfect copies of an errant text, we would still not know which parts we could trust and which we could not.

"Inerrancy Diverts Faith Away From Christ"

Finally, it has been objected that "the doctrine of inerrancy directs our attention away from the supreme focus of faith—Jesus Christ." In light of what we have already seen about Christ's own view of Scripture, however, it would seem that just the opposite is true. To *deny* inerrancy brings the authority of Christ into question and leaves our faith with no focus at all.

The basic reason for accepting Biblical inerrancy is that Jesus taught it. Our faith in Christ and our surrender to His lordship demand that we believe His word on *every* subject, including Scripture itself. The Jesus to whom we yield our hearts and minds is the same Jesus who says, "Scripture cannot be broken." This must be our confession too.

6

Reasons for Believing the Bible

Isaiah 41:21-26; 44:24-45:7; Luke 3:1, 2

Thus far we have been attempting to present the Bible's own view of itself. We have outlined the Biblical doctrines of revelation, inspiration, and inerrancy. We have not asked whether it is true, but have more or less assumed that if the Bible teaches it, it *must* be true.

It is time to pause and question this assumption. Why do we believe something just because it is taught in the Bible? We could say that we believe it because the Bible is the Word of God, and therefore true and inerrant. But why do we believe it *is* the Word of God? It *claims* to be the Word of God, and therefore true and inerrant; but *any* writing or any person could make such a claim. Just claiming it does not make it true. There must be reasons for accepting the claim.

We must be careful not to argue in a circle. It is not enough to say, "I believe the Bible because it is the Word of God, and I believe it is the Word of God because it says so." We must be able to present *specific reasons* for believing that the Bible is the Word of God. That is the purpose of this chapter.

44

The Unity of the Bible

We are so accustomed to seeing and using the Bible as a single volume that we take its unity for granted. "Why shouldn't it be bound as one volume?" we ask. "It is just one book, isn't it?" Yes, it is; but that answer is not as obvious and unimportant as it may seem at first.

What makes the Bible's unity so remarkable is its great *diversity.* There are, after all, sixty-six separate units, written over a time span of about fifteen hundred years. Around forty authors were involved, writing in three languages. A wide variety of writing is included, such as history, law, poetry, prophecy, biography, and letters.

Despite the diversity of these sixty-six parts, they do indeed fit together into a single unified book. Although many aspects of this unity could be mentioned, we will focus upon the main one: the unity of the Bible's *theme.*

Within the pages of the Bible a single main theme is being developed: the drama of redemption, the story of one great planned rescue operation. Despite the diversity of its separate units, the Bible tells this one story. There is a single plot being worked out; every section has its place in the unfolding of this plot. There is a beginning, a middle, and an end.

Sometimes this unity is called *organic,* because the story grows like a living organism, like a plant growing to maturity. The roots are seen in Genesis; the rest of the Old Testament is the stem. The Gospels, which present the life and work of Christ, are the flower. Acts and the epistles describe the fruit, which is the church. The harvest is pictured in the book of Revelation.

The question that must be asked is this: in light of the Bible's great diversity, how can we explain this remarkable unity? What could have caused it? It is an accepted axiom of rational thinking that every effect must have sufficient cause. Not just any cause will do; the cause must be sufficient to produce the observed effect.

What is sufficient to explain the unity of the Bible? We must rule out chance; it is obvious that an intelligent purpose or plan is involved. Could a human mind be behind this plan? The great span of time rules this out. The unity requires a single mind behind the whole Bible, and no human being could have supervised a fifteen-hundred-year project such as this.

Also it must be pointed out that this exciting drama is not simply a piece of literature. It is not just on paper; it actually happened in history. The story unfolds not just on the pages of a book, but in actual lives and events in history. This gives an even deeper dimension to the unity of the Bible. It requires not just an author who could produce such a book, but also a director who could actually bring these things to pass in history, who could carry out a single plan involving several thousand years.

What is sufficient to explain it all? The only satisfactory answer is that both the plan and the book are of *divine* origin. Only the all-knowing, all-powerful God, who transcends history and to whom a thousand years is as but a day, could have written this drama on the pages of history and then caused such a varied collection of writings to tell it as one story. This is one reason why we believe the Bible's own testimony to its origin, that it is indeed the Word of God.

Fulfilled Prophecies

Another reason why we believe the Bible is from God is the pattern of fulfilled prophecies woven into its fabric. Its writers record numerous predictions of events that later actually happened. Such successful prophecies are evidence of supernatural knowledge and supernatural power at work, for only God has infallible knowledge of the future.

God himself is willing to let His claims stand or fall by the test of fulfilled prophecy, and He challenges any would-be ''gods'' to do the same.

"Present your case," the Lord says.
"Bring forward your strong arguments," the King
of Jacob says.
Let them bring forth and declare to us what is going
to take place;
As for the former events, declare what they were,
That we may consider them, and know their out-
come;
Or announce to us what is coming.
Declare the things that are going to come after-
ward,
That we may know that you are gods (Isaiah 41:21-
23; see verse 26).

This is one reason why the Bible contains so many
prophecies. They are given so that their fulfillment may
establish the divine origin of the Scriptural message. As
Jesus put it, "From now on I am telling you before it
comes to pass, so that when it does occur, you may believe that I am He" (John 13:19).

Of the great number of fulfilled prophecies in the Bible,
only a few will be mentioned here. One of the most remarkable of all is Ezekiel's prediction about the downfall
of the city of Tyre (Ezekiel 26). The prophecy, written in
the sixth century B.C., was fulfilled in detail at the hands
of Alexander's Greek army in the late fourth century B.C.

Another prophecy is Isaiah's prediction that God would
use a ruler named Cyrus to rebuild the fallen city of
Jerusalem (Isaiah 44:28—45:7). Two centuries later
Cyrus, king of Persia, sent the Jews home from their
Babylonian captivity, especially instructing them to re-
build the temple in Jerusalem (Ezra 1:1-3).

Concerning Jesus it was accurately predicted that He
would be born in Bethlehem (Micah 5:2). In Psalm
22:11-21, David gives so striking a description of the
crucifixion of Jesus that it sounds like an eyewitness report. Yet he, like Micah, wrote centuries before Christ!

47

There are literally hundreds of other such prophecies in the Bible. They are not just ambiguous, generalized, short-term guesses. They are broad in scope, precise in detail, and long-ranging in time.

Again working from the principle of sufficient cause, we conclude that the only possible cause or origin of this interwoven prophetic material is God himself. This confirms our belief that Scripture is the Word of God.

The Bible's Remarkable Accuracy

If the Bible is the inerrant Word of God, then we would expect it to be true in every place where it is possible for us to test it. Nothing less would be consistent with the claims it makes for itself.

When we do in fact put the Bible to the test, what is the result? We find that it is remarkably and consistently accurate in every way.

Internal Consistency

One way in which the Bible demonstrates its accuracy is that it does not contradict itself. It is internally consistent. This is quite amazing, in light of the great diversity discussed above.

The greatest test of this type of accuracy lies in the many parallel descriptions of the same events, such as in the Gospels. Because these accounts are not given from the same perspective, it may appear at first that contradictions exist. Careful study shows that this is not the case, however. From the very earliest Christian centuries, scholars have compiled "harmonies" of the Gospels, showing how the evangelists agree with each other.

Historical Accuracy

The Bible is *historical* through and through. It makes innumerable allusions to historical events and characters. These are described as things that actually happened and people who truly lived. Through the wealth of data uncovered by historical and archeological research, we are able to measure the Bible's historical accuracy. In every case where its claims can be thus tested, the Bible proves to be accurate and reliable.

In the nineteenth century, when negative Biblical criticism was at its height, the common practice was to dismiss the bulk of the Bible's historical material as myth or legend or fiction. For instance, the critics denied that such people as Abraham or the Hittite nation ever existed. They boldly asserted that Moses could not have written the Pentateuch because no one knew how to write then! They declared that the book of Acts was a fictional narrative written by an unknown author in the mid-second century.

Much to the critics' embarrassment, however, a steady stream of archeological discoveries has swept away such unfounded attacks and has left the Biblical accounts standing reliable and true and solid. The culture and customs of Abraham's day, just as described in the Bible, have been confirmed by such findings. The great Hittite empire, previously unknown except in the Bible, was dramatically brought to light by the archeologist Winckler in 1906. Such incidents could be multiplied.

The accuracy of Scripture as established by such investigation does not of itself prove that the Bible is the Word of God. It is certainly *one* of the necessary pillars supporting this claim, however, since only total accuracy is consistent with divine origin. If it is the Word of God, we would expect it to be without error in these areas open to our investigation. If we could not trust it in these areas, how could we trust it in those matters which we cannot test?

In this chapter we have briefly examined three reasons why we accept the Bible's claims to be the Word of God and therefore true and inerrant. There are still other reasons, the principal one of which will be presented in the next chapter.

7

Jesus' Resurrection and its Implications

John 2:13-22; Acts 13:30-39; Romans 1:1-4

The strongest, most convincing reason for believing that the Bible is God's inerrant Word is that *Jesus said so,* as we saw in chapter 1. But now we must ask ourselves, why do we accept the authority of Jesus' word? How can we establish His authority without arguing in a circle? It is not enough to say, "We believe the Bible is the Word of God because Jesus, the very Son of God, says so;and we believe Jesus is the Son of God because the Bible says so."

The answer is found in the fact that Jesus rose from the dead. By using ordinary methods of historical investigation, we can establish that fact. The resurrection in turn establishes Jesus' authority and thus the truthfulness of His claims.

This is not circular reasoning, because we do not presuppose anything in particular about the nature of the Biblical records. We approach them as if they were just ordinary documents making certain claims. We examine these records as we would any other document in order to decide whether its claims are true.

When we approach the Bible on this basis, the first thing that impresses us is the over-all reliability of the records. (See the last point in chapter 6.) Not only do they have the "ring of truth," as J. B. Phillips says: they are also constantly being verified by new archeological discoveries. This is especially true of the New Testament records.

Our primary interest, though, is in the assertion that Jesus was raised from the dead. Regarding this claim we ask two questions: (1) What proves the resurrection? (2) What does the resurrection prove?

What Proves the Resurrection?

To establish the case for the resurrection, we only need to evaluate the Gospel records in the same way we examine any other ancient document. In fact, the only thing we need to presuppose is the universally accepted principle of sufficient cause. This is the simple and obvious rule that every effect has a cause that is sufficient to bring it into existence. In relation to the resurrection of Christ the argument is simply this: the only *sufficient* cause for certain admitted effects is the resurrection of Jesus.

We may consider first the indisputable fact of the disciples' testimony to the empty tomb. The effect that demands an explanation is simply their testimony that the tomb was empty. What could have caused them to give such a report? After all possible explanations have been considered, the principle of sufficient cause drives us to conclude that the reports of the empty tomb can be explained only by the actual resurrection.

Of course, many other supposedly sufficient explanations have been offered, but when examined they are insufficient and inconsistent with all available data. It has been suggested, for instance, that the disciples just lied about the tomb's being empty. But this is contrary to their high moral character and teaching. It is also contrary to their willingness to suffer persecution and death in defense of their report. Besides, whether it was true or not could easily have been checked by neutral or even hostile parties. Thus this suggestion is inadequate.

Some say the disciples went to the wrong tomb: the empty tomb that they saw was not the one Jesus was really buried in. But this explanation also ignores reality. The records show that the disciples knew where the tomb was. Also, the number of people involved precludes the possibility that *all* would be mistaken—even the owner of the tomb! Besides, the officials would have quickly corrected such an error.

Others say that the tomb really was empty, but only because Jesus was still alive when He was laid in it. He revived, got out of the tomb, and died later—so they say.

Such a suggestion is insufficient because it is contrary to all the available data relating to Jesus' death and burial. The records show that He was weak from sleeplessness, scourging, and crucifixion. His side had been pierced; and it yielded blood and water, which is an indication of death (John 19:34). An experienced Roman centurion witnessed and certified the death (Mark 15:39, 44, 45). Burial consisted of being tightly wrapped in strips of cloth packed with seventy-five to a hundred pounds of spices (John 19:39, 40). A huge stone blocked the tomb, and a guard was at the entrance (Matthew 27:66). Now the question is, could a man in such a state and under such conditions, even if He had been alive at burial, have been *able* to exit from the tomb? Even if He had got out, could He have had the necessary psychological impact on His disciples to fill them with the zeal they later had?

Others try to explain the reports of the empty tomb by saying that Jesus' body was stolen. But this is quite improbable. His enemies lacked the inclination to steal it. Also, if they had done so, it would have been to their advantage to produce the body later in order to disprove the disciples' claims. On the other hand, Jesus' friends lacked both the inclination and the opportunity to steal the body. A guard blocked their way. The fact that the graveclothes remained neatly intact (John 20:4-7) is inconsistent with a hasty theft.

In the end there is only one circumstance that is sufficient to explain the reports of the empty tomb, namely, the actual resurrection of Jesus.

Along with the reports of the empty tomb is another fact that demands an explanation, namely, the disciples' testimony concerning the appearances of Christ after His death and burial. What could have caused them to say they had seen the risen Lord if indeed they had not? Again, several suggestions have been offered, but the only one consistent with the principle of sufficient cause is the reality of the resurrection itself.

For instance, some have claimed that the reports of the appearances are the result of "wish fulfillment": the disciples' intense desire to see the risen Lord caused them to have hallucinations. It would appear, however, that their psychological state was just the opposite of what would be necessary for such a thing. They were not expecting the resurrection, and they were far from optimistic. In fact, they had given up hope. They were filled with disbelief, sorrow, and discouragement. They were hardly gullible: they failed to recognize Christ in His early appearances, and the earliest reports were rejected as untrue. See Mark 16:9-14; Luke 24:11-31; John 20:1-2, 11-31; 21:4-23.

The circumstances, number, and variety of the appearances also rule out the idea of hallucinations. Jesus often appeared to many people at once. Also, the appearances were "not fleeting glimpses, but prolonged interviews" (Orr). Such an explanation also leaves the empty tomb unexplained.

Some have suggested that Christ did not actually arise from the dead bodily, but that He did live on and appear to His disciples in a mystical, psychic manner. That is, it was not His real body that they saw, but rather a kind of apparition. Again, this is not consistent with the data available. The body the disciples saw could be touched (Luke 24:36-43). The risen Christ ate food in their presence to prove that He was not a mere apparition. It must be remembered, too, that the tomb was empty.

It is sometimes suggested that the disciples lied about the appearances. Would this be congruous with their general character and teaching? Would this be compatible with their later zeal and readiness to face martyrdom? Would they have risked their lives for a known lie? Besides, the tomb was empty.

After all things have been considered, the reports of the resurrection appearances of Jesus can be sufficiently explained only by the resurrection itself.

The phenomena of the empty tomb and the post-resurrection appearances of Jesus have long been considered as the two main lines of evidence for the resurrection. But there are others. For instance, the establishment and rapid growth of the church defy all explanation apart from Jesus' resurrection. His disciples were in no state of mind following His death to launch such an enterprise with the zeal and conviction necessary to conquer an empire. Only His resurrection could have given them the impetus to build a kingdom of such scope and endurance.

Another fact unexplainable apart from the resurrection of Jesus is the very faith of the apostles, especially as contrasted with their state of mind prior to the resurrection. Given their unbelief and despair, what besides the resurrection could have changed them overnight into men of faith and courage? The same is true of the conversion of Saul of Tarsus into Paul the apostle.

Thus we have no choice. We *must* accept the reality of the resurrection, because it is the only sufficient cause for a number of indisputable facts.

What Does the Resurrection Prove?

Granting the fact of the resurrection, our next question is this: what does it prove? The answer is that it establishes the divine authority and trustworthiness of Jesus. He claimed to speak God's own word (John 7:16), and He set forth the promised fact of His own resurrection as the conclusive proof of His claims (John 2:18-22; Matthew 12:38-40; 16:4).

The resurrection shows that Jesus was who He claimed to be, namely, the Son of God himself (Romans 1:1-4). It therefore establishes the truth of everything He ever said. Because of the Bible's proven reliability in recording historical data, we have no reason to doubt that Jesus actually said the things attributed to Him in the Gospels. Therefore we accept them as true. This includes all His teaching about the nature of the Bible: "Scripture cannot be broken" (John 10:35), and the rest.

Thus it should not surprise us that when Jesus was raised from the dead, His disciples remembered that He had promised it; *"and they believed the Scripture, and the word which Jesus had spoken"* (John 2:22). This is exactly what we should do.

In these last two chapters we have only briefly examined the basic reasons why we accept the Bible as God's inerrant Word. Together they form a solid foundation for our confidence in its every teaching and our surrender to its authority.

8

Dealing With Difficulties
in the Bible

Psalm 119:41-48, 89, 129, 130
Romans 1:18-28

We have suggested that the Bible claims to be and proves to be the inerrant Word of God. If this is true, and if the case for it is so clear-cut, why doesn't everyone recognize it immediately and acknowledge its authority?

One reason is that in our present text of the Bible there are what are called "difficulties" or "problem passages" or "alleged discrepancies." That is, there are certain phenomena which seem at first to contradict the claim that the Bible is inerrant. Those who reject Biblical authority are constantly appealing to these phenomena, and believers are sometimes caught off guard and have their faith severely shaken when confronted with them.

Our purpose in this chapter is to present certain *guiding principles* for handling objections to belief in the Bible as God's inerrant Word. We cannot discuss each objection that may be raised, but we can offer principles that the believer can learn and apply as needed.

1. *The strong positive case in favor of belief puts any difficulty on the defensive and creates the presumption that it has a solution.*

Suppose that one of your very close friends is arrested. You have known him for years as a person of deep Christian faith and high moral character. Yet he is charged with burglary. "Wait a minute," you say. "I know my friend. He simply would not do this. There must be some mistake. There must be some other explanation."

This is precisely our response whenever we hear an objection to the Bible: "Wait a minute. I know this book. The marks of divine origin are obvious in its pages. It has a remarkable record of accuracy. Accusations have been hurled against it before, and they have proved to be false. This must be the case now. This objection must be based on some misunderstanding. Let us see how we can clear it up."

Many are quick to indict and condemn the Bible at the least suggestion of error. This is inconsistent with its overall character, however. We must give the benefit of the doubt to the Bible, and presume that a solution is possible.

2. *Many so-called difficulties are quite superficial; a reasonable explanation is usually available to anyone who will take the trouble to look for it.*

We must not be content merely to rest on the presumption that difficulties can be resolved; we must examine the problem to see if indeed a solution can be found. When this is done, the difficulty usually turns out to be superficial and the explanation quite simple.

In a local high school one year, the senior honors class was studying various philosophies of life. The Christian faith was often spoken of disparagingly by the teacher and many of the students. A Christian in the class complained, and the teacher said, "If you want to, you may invite someone in to speak on behalf of the Bible."

The student approached his minister, who is a good friend of mine, and asked him to visit the class. The young minister was quite fearful of the problems he might have to deal with, but he consented. With trepidation he faced the class, and instantly a bright young skeptic began the attack. "Here's a question you can't answer, preacher," he said confidently. *"Where did Cain get his wife?"* From that point on, my preacher friend knew he had nothing to fear.

This is a good example of the superficial nature of many perennial Bible difficulties. A person may know that Adam and Eve had two sons named Cain and Abel (and later a third named Seth), and assume that these were the *only* children and thus the only people in the world. Thus when Cain's wife is mentioned (Genesis 4:17), he jumps to the conclusion that this must be a phony story. The answer is simple and readily available, though. Genesis 5:4 specifically says that Adam and Eve had other children, including daughters. They are just not named in the text.

Another example is the difference between Matthew 3:17 and Luke 3:22. Each is reporting what God said from Heaven at the baptism of Jesus. Matthew puts it in third person: "This is my beloved Son"; Luke puts it in second person: "Thou art my beloved Son." Is this a discrepancy? No, not when we understand that the writers often recorded sayings and events in indirect discourse, summary, or paraphrase. In this case Matthew seems to be reporting in indirect discourse while Luke gives the direct quotation.

The difference between Matthew 20:30 and Mark 10:46, 47 is often brought up. Matthew says that Jesus healed two blind men at Jericho; Mark says He healed a blind man named Bartimaeus. Were there two, or one? No doubt there were two, but Bartimaeus was the leader and spokesman. Thus he is the one Mark concentrates on. (Note that Mark does not say "one and only one blind man.") This also applies to Mark 16:5 and Luke 24:4.

Many, many difficulties can be dealt with in just this manner. Reasonable explanations are available if one wants to find them.

3. *Most if not all difficulties are due to incomplete or erroneous understanding, either of Scripture itself or of the world around us.*

Sometimes in preparation for stressing this point, I have informed my audience of the following fact: I married three sisters, divorced none, and all are still living. Many people refuse to believe it, thinking it more charitable to brand me a liar than a bigamist!

The statement *is* true, and no bigamy has occurred. One sister is my wife; I performed the wedding ceremonies for the other two. It was merely erroneous understanding that led to the charge of error or falsehood.

This is what happens often in relation to the Bible. We must remember that, though the Bible is infallible, we are not. Our interpretations are often mistaken.

Sometimes a faulty understanding of the Bible itself leads to difficulties. For instance, it is common today for critics to ridicule the accounts of the ascension of Jesus. Such a story shows, they say, that the Bible writers held to the erroneous idea of a three-layered universe with "Heaven" as the top tier. Jesus supposedly is pictured as zooming up, up, and away until He reaches that layer.

This is, of course, a false reading of the text. Jesus did ascend, but into a *cloud* (Acts 1:9). A knowledge of Bible history should lead us to infer that this is no ordinary cloud, but rather the very presence of God manifested in the form of a cloud (see Exodus 40:34-38; Matthew 17:5). After Jesus had been received into the cloud, both He and it probably faded away.

Some see a problem in the different reports of John the Baptist's preaching. According to the King James Version, in Matthew he declares that he is not worthy to *bear* Jesus' shoes (3:11); in Luke he says he is not worthy to *unloose* them (3:16). Is one of the Gospels wrong? No. In his preaching John probably referred many times to his unworthiness in relation to Jesus' shoes, sometimes saying one thing and sometimes another.

For another example, some are troubled by the apparent contradiction between 2 Samuel 24:1 and 1 Chronicles 21:1. Samuel says that *the Lord* incited King David to take a census in Israel; Chronicles says that *Satan* moved him to do so.

Is this not a blatant contradiction? No, not when we understand the relation between Satan's activities and God's permissive sovereignty. In Job 1:12-19 and 1 Kings 22:19-23, we see that God may *allow* Satan to tempt or test His servants, though always within limits (see 1 Corinthians 10:13). This is no doubt the solution to the apparent discrepancy.

We should note also that difficulties sometimes arise from incomplete or faulty understanding of the world itself. Some scientists still believe that the theory of evolution explains the origin of man; thus they declare the Bible's account of creation to be erroneous. However, many other scientists—believers and unbelievers alike—have concluded that the concept of evolution is not supported by the evidence.

We must resist the temptation to ascribe infallibility to pronouncements made in the name of science. A well-known caution is the fact that in 1861 the French Academy of Science issued a list of fifty-one scientific "truths" that disprove the Bible. Each of the fifty-one "truths" has since been disproved!

Considering our finitude and our fallibility, whenever we are confronted with an alleged error in the Bible, we should first question our own understanding.

4. *Human inability to solve certain problems does not mean that they have no solution.*

There are times when we may have to admit that we cannot find an adequate solution to an alleged discrepancy in the Bible. In such cases it is perfectly legitimate to reserve judgment and trust that there *is* a solution, and that it may come to light in the future. This applies to certain problems involving Old Testament numbers.

Why should we not feel threatened by our inability to solve some difficulties? Because in the past, time after time, new discoveries in areas such as history or linguistics have produced solutions to such problems. Supposed errors have been shown to be facts: the Bible was correct after all!

For instance, critics at one time questioned the claim of 1 Kings 9:26, that Solomon had a seaport at Eziongeber. No rationale for such a facility was evident. But archeologists later discovered a huge copper works in the area, thus justifying the need for a seaport and validating the Bible's claim.

The consistent pattern of similar discoveries gives us confidence that solutions to continuing problems do exist, even if we are unable to find them now.

5. *Even though the Christian has difficulties, the unbeliever has more and greater ones.*

No world view is completely free from difficulties and unsolved problems. The unbeliever, for instance, may reject the Bible's teaching that God created the universe. But then he is left with the problem of explaining the origin of things. When God is excluded, the only option remaining is *chance*. The idea that chance can account for this present universe is far more incredible than creation.

The unbeliever's biggest difficulty, though, is how to explain Jesus' testimony to the inerrancy of Scripture if indeed it cannot be trusted. The words of Jesus— *Scripture cannot be broken* —continue to be the undoing of every denial, the stone of stumbling for every contrary theory. For the believer, though, they remain the solid foundation for his confidence in God's inerrant Word.

9

The Sufficiency of the Bible

Deuteronomy 4:1, 2; Mark 7:1-13
Psalm 119:103-105, 127, 128

Most of us have seen reproductions of some of the early Sears, Roebuck catalogues. One of the most impressive things about them was their completeness. Some editions included practically everything necessary for everyday life, including medicine, automobiles, and even houses! Regarding material needs, they were all-sufficient.

The Bible that God has given us is likewise all-sufficient for meeting our *spiritual* needs. It is important that we understand this. It should make us want to search the Scriptures more. It should also keep us from seeking elsewhere for answers to our spiritual problems. Hence in this chapter our subject is the *sufficiency* of the Bible.

Sola Scriptura

One of the great slogans of the Protestant Reformation was *sola scriptura,* or "Scripture alone!" In spiritual matters the Bible is fully sufficient to answer every question and fill every need. As Martin Luther said, "All that God has done, particularly all that pertains to our salvation, is clearly put down and noted in Scripture''; ''all that we are to believe, aye, more than enough, is in Scripture.''

Others have declared the Bible to be the ''all-sufficient rule of faith and practice.'' This means first that it is sufficient as a source of truth (''rule of faith''). All Scripture, says Paul, is ''profitable for teaching'' (2 Timothy 3:16). Jesus promised that the Holy Spirit would guide the apostles into ''all truth'' (John 16:13), or all truth necessary for our life and salvation. Other things could have been included, but faith can rest firmly on what is there (John 20:31).

As a sufficient ''rule of practice,'' the Bible is ''profitable . . . for reproof, for correction, for training in righteousness; that the man of God may be adequate, equipped for every good work'' (2 Timothy 3:16, 17). It casts light on every problem; it guides us in every area of life. Its principles apply to every decision; it gives the perfect pattern for the church. The Bible truly is ''a lamp to my feet, and a light to my path'' (Psalm 119:105).

Sola scriptura means that Scripture alone is an *adequate* source of truth and moral knowledge, but it means more. It means that Scripture alone is *the authoritative* source of such truth and knowledge. Because of its unique nature as the inspired, inerrant Word of God, Scripture is the sole norm, the ultimate and final authority for faith and life.

False Standards of Authority

A constant danger for the church is the tendency to supplement or even displace Scripture with false norms. We can resist this tendency by being aware of the Bible's perennial rivals and by jealously guarding against all efforts to elevate them to a position of authority.

Tradition

One of the most persistent challengers of Biblical authority is human tradition. A tradition usually begins innocently enough as a particular interpretation or application of Scripture. Through the years, however, this human interpretation is gradually elevated in importance until it comes to be viewed as having authority independent of Scripture and alongside it.

By the time Christ Jesus came into the world, the Jews had accumulated a large body of tradition which they slavishly followed and taught as if it were the Word of God itself. In fact (as usually happens), it had become even more important and binding than the Bible.

One day the Pharisees chastised Jesus because He and His disciples did not always wash their hands before eating, as "the tradition of the elders" required. Turning the tables, Jesus pointed out how the Pharisees actually paid more attention to their traditions than to the Bible. "You . . . set aside the commandment of God in order to keep your tradition," He said (Mark 7:1-13).

By the sixteenth century the Roman Catholic Church had accumulated a similar body of tradition, including the official doctrine that such things as the pronouncements of councils and popes were of equal authority with the Bible. The Reformation doctrine of *sola Scriptura* was directed against this misuse of tradition.

The problem is still with us today. The Catholic Church still formally places its traditions alongside the Bible. Many of the Protestant denominations that decry this practice have allowed their own man-made creeds to usurp the Bible's authority. And even among those of us who are non-creedal, certain patterns of worship and service have a way of becoming untouchable, as if they were instituted by God himself.

Why, for instance, must the midweek service always be on Wednesday? Does every preaching service have to end with an invitation hymn? Is there only one way to make the "good confession"? Does the Sunday worship service have to be before noon? Must the Lord's Supper always precede the sermon?

Traditional practices are not necessarily wrong, of course. What is wrong, and what must be avoided, is elevating fallible human applications of Biblical principles to the level of Scripture itself. Scripture alone has binding authority.

Personal Experience or Opinion

One of Satan's most successful devices is to convince a person that his own subjective experiences or his own judgments and opinions are more important and more authoritative than God's own Word. Satan was able to persuade Eve that she knew as much about reality and morality as God did (Genesis 3:1-6). He still continues to convince the gullible that God's voice is insufficient, that they must also hear and heed the voice of reason or conscience, or inner mystical voices of some kind.

The sixteenth century Reformers had to contend not only against the Catholic Church, but also against a whole assortment of mystics, spiritualists, and rationalists. These were men who judged Scripture by their own mystical experiences, new "revelations," or rationalistic opinions. Since they thus implied that the Bible was an insufficient guide, the *sola scriptura* theme was directed against them also.

Ascribing ultimate authority to personal experience has produced many religious groups that still flourish today. A basic Quaker belief is that God continues to give new revelations through a mystical "inner light" that is present in every person. Mormonism is based on an alleged angelic visitation to Joseph Smith. Ellen G. White, founder of Seventh-Day Adventism, had numerous visions confirming her doctrines. An "angelic" vision to Herbert W. Armstrong's wife persuaded him that his religious system was correct; the result was the Worldwide Church of God. Pentecostalism and modern charismatics interpret certain experiences as "new revelations" from God.

A less mystical but perhaps more common challenge to the Bible's sole authority is something that may be called "*I*-thinkism." This occurs when one either ignores or challenges the teaching of God's Word on a particular subject and says, "Now, *I* think . . ." For instance, judgments are often pronounced on grave social and moral issues with no apparent awareness of what the Bible says about them. As one person said, "I think homosexual activity is OK, since that's the way God made those people." (See Genesis 1:27, 31; Romans 1:21-32.) A preacher's wife once said, "I think capital punishment is wrong because it is not administered fairly." She preferred her judgment to the Bible's (see Genesis 9:5, 6; Exodus 21:12; Romans 13:1-4). A Sunday-school class was discussing whether women should teach men. First Timothy 2:12-15 was read, and one person said, "I know that is what the Bible says, but I think it's all right anyway."

The common element in all of these examples is the idea that the Bible is not a sufficient guide, and that it must be supplemented by something from within ourselves. Subjective experiences and the exercise of reason thus take precedence over Biblical authority.

Consistent Christianity, however, demands that we exclude every false norm and false standard of authority, and submit ourselves to the Bible alone. Only the Bible is God's inspired and inerrant Word, and it truly is a sufficient rule of faith and practice.

Aids to Understanding

Recognizing the Bible's sufficiency as the sole *norm* for faith and life does not mean that we exclude and ignore completely the use of human reason, traditions, and interpretations. On the contrary, we should continue to use them even more than ever, but only as *aids* to *understanding* the Bible and applying it to our lives, not as authoritative norms.

In my early childhood my family attended a church where the Sunday-school classes used nothing but the Bible as a study text. There is nothing wrong with this, of course; there is no better book to study. This church, however, had concluded that it was *wrong* to study from any source other than the Bible. Only *God's* Word, not human words, should be our guide. (The fact that the Sunday-school teachers explained the Bible in their own human words did not seem to bother them.)

This congregation's problem was that it did not see the difference between a *norm* and an *aid to understanding*. Books, commentaries, sermons, lessons, and informed opinions and interpretations of all kinds may help us to understand the meaning of the Bible, even though the Bible alone is the final authority. We do not use such things in order to judge the Bible; the Bible must always judge them.

The Bible is indeed a mine laden with wonderful treasures that we can extract, using as tools our own reason and the fruit of the study and labor of others. Once we have made these treasures our own, we will find them sufficient for our every need.

10

Understanding the Bible

Nehemiah 8:1-12; Matthew 13:14, 15, 18-23

On one occasion when Jesus was teaching, "He called to Himself the multitude, and said to them, 'Hear, and understand' " (Matthew 15:10). This admonition applies to all that God has spoken: "Read, and understand."

The Bible *is* the Word of God, and it *is* the authoritative norm and judge of our lives, whether we acknowledge it or not. But it will guide us properly only when we understand what it says. God himself has given us the Bible; it is our responsibility to read and study it until we understand it.

In this chapter we will emphasize the fact that the Bible *can* be understood. We will discuss the various sources of help available to those who pursue such study. Finally, we will enumerate a few basic rules for interpreting Scripture properly.

The Clarity of Scripture

Occasionally someone will question whether it is even *possible* to understand the Bible. This doubt often arises from the fact that there are so many varying interpretations, so many disagreements over the meaning of Scripture. "If even the best scholars cannot agree on what the Bible says, how can I ever understand it?" is the cry.

At other times this doubt has a more philosophical basis. It is suggested that there will always be a gap between our understanding of Scripture and what God really meant, simply because human language cannot express divine thoughts or because our understanding is always distorted by personal prejudices. Anyone who makes an issue of a particular interpretation is then accused of "creating divisions" with his "party dogma" or "sectarian interpretation."

By the sixteenth century the Catholic Church had decided that the Bible is too obscure to be interpreted properly by the ordinary layman. Hence it limited the interpretation and even the reading of the Bible to the clergy. Against this idea the Reformers stressed the *clarity* of Scripture. Even though some parts are more difficult to understand than others, the Bible's message of salvation is clear and accessible to all.

We affirm the clarity of Scripture because we believe that God is able to communicate with man. When God speaks to us (Hebrews 1:1, 2), He certainly desires to be understood. Surely the sovereign, all-knowing God is competent to speak so that He *can* be understood. Isaiah 55:11 says that He does not speak in vain: "So shall My word be which goes forth from My mouth; it shall not return to Me empty, without accomplishing what I desire, and without succeeding in the matter for which I sent it."

Human language is no barrier to God. We are made in His image (Genesis 1:26, 27); our thought-processes are not alien to Him. The words and messages of the Bible truly represent what is in God's mind, and our minds can grasp their true meanings.

Even a sinner's mind is able to understand the basic message of the gospel. The sinner can come to faith in Jesus through the reading or preaching of the Word. This is true by God's design: "These have been *written* that you may believe that Jesus is the Christ, the Son of God" (John 20:31). "So faith comes from hearing, and hearing by the word of Christ" (Romans 10:17).

This does not mean, of course, that study of the Word is unnecessary. The Word is like a mine of precious jewels. Certain gems of truth are plain and clear on the surface; others lie at deeper levels. The latter *can* be attained, but honest and diligent effort is required. The clarity of Scripture assures us that such effort will not be in vain.

Resources To Aid Understanding

Being in the image of God means that we have the inherent intellectual capacity to understand God's Word. Still, God does not expect us to retire like monks to our individual cells and study in isolation without any help whatsoever. There are resources available, both human and divine, to aid us.

On the human level God has provided *teachers.* As the Ethiopian eunuch was reading from Isaiah, God sent Philip to be his teacher. Philip asked, "Do you understand what you are reading?" The eunuch replied, "Well, how could I, unless someone guides me?" (Acts 8:30, 31).

Because this need for guidance is shared by all, God has established the office or role of teacher (or pastor-teacher). See Romans 12:7; 1 Corinthians 12:28, 29; Ephesians 4:11-16. This seems to be the special responsibility of the elders (1 Timothy 3:2; Titus 1:9-11; Ephesians 4:11). In general, those who are strong or mature in the faith should teach the younger or weaker until they themselves are capable of teaching others (Hebrews 5:11-14; 2 Timothy 2:2).

To ignore this distinction between the teacher and the taught not only is contrary to God's established plan; it also delays or even prevents a proper understanding of

Scripture. Many small group Bible studies proceed without a qualified teacher; each person reads a verse and tells "what it means to me." Despite the good intentions and satisfied feelings, little learning takes place.

Understanding Scripture must proceed in two steps. Before anything else, one must ask, "What does it *mean?*" What is the actual meaning of the verse or passage? It cannot mean something different to each person; it must mean only what the original writer intended it to mean. This is usually something that cannot be perceived "on the spur of the moment" or without guided study. Here is where a teacher is especially needed: to explain what the Bible author intends to say and why he says it.

The second step is the legitimate question, "What does it mean *to me?*" How does this passage, properly understood, apply to my daily life? This is indeed a question that should be discussed by the whole group, including the teacher. But here we are talking about application, not interpretation. We cannot know the application ("what it means to me") of a passage until we know its proper interpretation ("what it means").

Local churches should be diligent and deliberate in providing teachers trained in the knowledge of the Word of God. Teachers should be knowledgeable especially in Bible history, Bible introduction, and Bible doctrine. Specific training courses should be provided in these areas if necessary. The resources of our Bible colleges and seminaries and their teachers can and should be used more effectively in the local educational program.

Anyone seeking understanding of Scripture should thus take advantage of what human teachers can provide. This includes the use of books and written aids of various kinds, as well as personal instruction.

This does not mean that we should accept uncritically whatever a teacher or book says. We are not at the mercy of any teacher; we can and should measure his teaching carefully by the Bible itself. The Berean Jews were praised for "examining the Scriptures daily" to see if even the apostle Paul's teaching was Biblical (Acts 17:10, 11).

Some misunderstand Hebrews 8:10, 11 (quoting Jeremiah 31:33, 34) to mean that Christians do not need to be taught by others. This is not the meaning of the passage. It is referring to the difference between participating in the old covenant and participating in the new. One entered the old covenant by birth; hence he had to learn to know God after entering. The new covenant is different. Membership is by conscious choice and *new* birth; knowing the Lord is a prerequisite. This is why those under the new covenant do not have to be taught to know the Lord.

Besides human teachers, there is another resource for understanding Scripture, namely, God's providential aid. Here we are *not* referring to what is called "illumination by the Holy Spirit." Many Protestants have wrongly concluded that the Spirit opens man's eyes and enables him to see the proper meaning of Scripture. Many Christians share this error, usually through a misapplication of Scripture. Certain passages that refer only to *apostolic inspiration* are assumed to refer to all Christians. An example is John 16:13, which promises that the Spirit "will guide you into all the truth." The context shows that this refers specifically to the apostles. The same is true of John 14:26 and 1 Corinthians 2:11-16.

If such illumination came to every Christian directly from the Holy Spirit, there would be no need for teachers; contrary to what we have already seen. Besides, if the Spirit provides all Christians with the proper interpretation of Scripture, why is there no unanimity of understanding among believers?

In 1 John 2:27 the "anointing" is sometimes taken as referring to the Holy Spirit and His inner teaching, but this cannot be. If this were true, again, where is the unanimity of understanding? Also, it would make not only human teachers but even Scripture obsolete. The best understanding is that the "anointing" is the Word of God itself. Verses 14 and 24 show that this is what John is talking about. The verse teaches the *sufficiency* of Scripture as a source of authoritative doctrine. It does not exclude human teachers, but it shows that their teaching must be the interpretation and application of Scripture.

Thus we conclude that the Holy Spirit does not give understanding apart from the normal processes of learning.

Still, God will help us understand the Bible. How? Through His special *providential* aid in answer to prayer. He will not give us an immediate awareness of new knowledge, but He can sharpen our mental processes. He can help us to clear our preoccupied minds so that we can concentrate. He can help us to recall ideas already encountered. He can help us overcome willful blindness that may be preventing us from understanding His law (see Psalm 119:18). He can give us wisdom to apply what we learn to our lives (James 1:5). He can providentially lead us to others who can help us.

Such aid is not a substitute for study, nor is it a shortcut to Biblical understanding. We must still apply ourselves diligently, using all the help available, in order to uncover the deeper gems of Bible knowledge.

Principles of Interpretation

Since the Bible is a historical book written in human language, in order to understand it one must apply the rules and methods of interpretation that are relevant to any such writing. There are no esoteric or secret rules, nor are we free to devise arbitrary rules. Here are some basic principles:

a) Look for the commonsense meaning (not necessarily the literal one). Sometimes this is called the historico-grammatical method.

b) Recognize the particular literary form of the writing: is it history, poetry, a letter, or what?

c) Use all the helps available: lexicons (such as Vine's *Expository Dictionary)* and Bible dictionaries (not Webster's) to understand words, commentaries to understand passages, and various translations.

d) Do not try to make everything fit a preconceived idea. This is the way divisions and sects begin.

e) Put every passage in its proper historical context. The distinction between the old and new covenants is basic, especially the unique role of Israel as the preparation for Christ's coming. Of each writing, ask who wrote it, to whom, and why.

f) Interpret specific passages only in relation to the context of the book and section in which they occur.

Some additional principles are derived from the fact that the Bible is not *just* a human book, but is also the Word of God:

a) Approach it in a spirit of submission, realizing that it *is* the Word of God.

b) Pray for the providential aid described above.

c) Since the Bible is ultimately one book by one author, different references to the same subject will help to explain each other. Examine all references to a subject, using a concordance or topical Bible, and let Scripture interpret Scripture. Use the clearer passages to explain the more difficult.

11

Profitable for Doctrine

1 Timothy 4:13-16; Titus 1:9-14; 2:1, 7;
2 John 9-11; 3 John 3-8

The Bible has been called "the all-sufficient rule of faith and practice." In this expression the word *faith* refers to doctrine or teaching to be believed, and the word *practice* refers to commandments or principles of conduct to be obeyed.

Truly the Bible is the final authority for both, and this is the way we should use it. This is its intended purpose. Second Timothy 3:16 says that Scripture is "profitable for teaching," and also "for reproof, for correction, for training in righteousness." In this chapter we are concerned only with the first item, teaching. (We should keep in mind that the words *doctrine* and *teaching* mean exactly the same thing.)

The Importance of Doctrine

Why is doctrine so important? Because what we believe or accept as true determines everything else we do. Beliefs determine actions, and mistaken beliefs lead to disastrous actions. Many people have killed their friends with guns they truly believed to be empty. A person with cancer symptoms who refuses to visit a doctor and learn the truth may succumb to the disease. The person who refuses to believe that God exists will act accordingly and suffer the consequences.

The importance of knowing Bible doctrine is heightened even more when we realize that the Bible teaches truth not just about sin and salvation but about God, man, and the universe as a whole. The Bible presents a total world and life view, a comprehensive interpretation of everything that exists. All decisions and all deeds, directly or indirectly, are related to *what the Bible teaches,* and should be determined by it.

Despite this importance, there seems to be a great deal of indifference toward doctrine. It is neglected even in our churches. The great emphasis on church growth in many instances has sidelined doctrine and focused attention on practical methods or "how-to" helps. Churchgoers are hearing many sermons that entertain or give moralistic advice, but offer no spiritual nutrition. Edith Schaeffer compares them to "sawdust sandwiches."

Even some of our church leaders are speaking of doctrine as if it were irrelevant. Contrary to the original connotation of Scripture as the "rule of faith," many are saying that *faith* does not involve doctrine at all! We are told that "faith is not the correct understanding of orthodox doctrines, even God's doctrines." "Our faith is in a Person—Jesus the Christ—not in a series of propositions," says another writer; "faith is directed not to Scripture but to Christ." This either/or choice is also affirmed in this statement: "We are committed to Christ, not doctrine." The same writer says, "Truth is personal, not doctrinal." Another adds, "Matters of doctrine are not part of the foundation but belong to the superstructure of the Christian edifice."

Such statements are seriously misleading, not in what they affirm, but in what they deny. They affirm that our faith is in Jesus, and this is true. But they deny that our faith is in propositions or doctrines, and this denial is not correct. Biblical faith is directed *both* to Jesus Christ *and* to propositions or doctrines. We believe *in* Jesus (John 3:16) or *on* Jesus (Acts 16:31, King James Version). This is the *trust* aspect of faith. But there is another equally necessary aspect of faith, namely, assent to the truth of certain propositions. The Bible mentions some of these doctrines in particular. Hebrews 11:6 says that we must *believe that* God exists and that He rewards those who seek Him. Jesus said those who do not *believe that* He is who He claimed to be will die in their sins (John 8:24). John wrote his Gospel so that we may *believe that* Jesus is the Christ, the Son of God (John 20:31). Those who *believe that* God raised Jesus from the dead will be saved (Romans 10:9).

Besides these specific statements, we are instructed to believe the revealed truth in general. Jesus exhorts us to believe *the gospel* (Mark 1:15). He condemns the Jews for not believing *his words* (John 5:47). Paul expressed his faith in *all things written* in the law and prophets (Acts 24:14). Refusing to believe *the truth* brings judgment (2 Thessalonians 2:12, 13).

These references show the serious error in saying that faith has nothing to do with doctrine. The idea that the person of Christ can be separated from certain propositions or truths about Christ is irrational. The very reason we believe *in* Christ is that we believe certain things *about* Him. Otherwise how could we explain our faith in *Christ,* rather than in Buddha, or even Hitler?

We should also note that doctrine *is* part of the church's foundation, since the Christian edifice is "built upon the foundation of the apostles and prophets" (Ephesians 2:20). In what way could the apostles be the foundation of the church except through their teaching?

The Bible itself puts great stress on doctrine. Scripture is in the first place profitable for teaching, says Paul

(2 Timothy 3:16). The early Christians continually devoted themselves first of all to the apostles' teaching (Acts 2:42). Church leaders are exhorted to concentrate on doctrine. Paul tells Timothy to give attention to "exhortation and teaching." "Pay close attention," he says, "to yourself and to your teaching; . . . for as you do this you will insure salvation both for yourself and for those who hear you" (1 Timothy 4:13, 16). Special praise is given to the elders who labor "in the word and doctrine" (1 Timothy 5:17, King James Version).

If doctrine is one of the Bible's main emphases, shouldn't it be ours too—in our sermons, in our Sunday-school literature and lessons, in our youth programs, in our camp curricula, in our colleges, and in our homes?

The Importance of *Sound* Doctrine

One thing worse than no doctrine is false doctrine. Scripture teaches us to be concerned not only with doctrine, but also with *sound* doctrine. There is such a thing as truth, and there is such a thing as error. We can and must know the difference between them.

"Sound doctrine" is a clear Biblical concept. Paul tells Titus to "speak the things which are fitting for sound doctrine" and to be an example both of good deeds and of "purity in doctrine" (Titus 2:1, 7). He tells Timothy to "retain the standard of sound words" and to nourish himself on sound doctrine (2 Timothy 1:13; 1 Timothy 4:6). The time will come, he says, when people will refuse to listen to sound doctrine, but that only makes it more necessary to "preach the word" (2 Timothy 4:2, 3).

A parallel stress is the Bible's emphasis on *truth*. God "desires all men to be saved and to come to the knowledge of the truth" (1 Timothy 2:4). "Faith in the truth" is a necessary condition for salvation (2 Thessalonians 2:12, 13). John wrote that he is glad when Christians walk in the truth: "I have no greater joy than this, to hear of my children walking in the truth" (3 John 3, 4).

Contrary to truth or sound doctrine is error or false doctrine, which is severely condemned in the Bible. Basically, false doctrine is from Satan. Paul warns against "doctrines of demons" (1 Timothy 4:1). Those who oppose the truth are in "the snare of the devil" (2 Timothy 2:23-26), whose chief characteristic is falsehood (John 8:44). Satan's final assault will be a massive barrage of deceit and lies (2 Thessalonians 2:9-12; Revelation 20:8).

Teaching false doctrine is condemned (Galatians 1:6-9; 1 Timothy 6:3-5; 2 Peter 2:1-3). *Believing* false doctrine is also condemned (2 Peter 3:16, 17; 2 Thessalonians 2:10, 12), and so is *supporting* or encouraging false doctrine (2 John 9-11). We are commanded to test teachers to see if they are false prophets (1 John 4:1-3).

Elders especially have the dual responsibility of teaching sound doctrine and refuting false teachers (Titus 1:9-14).

What do we learn from the Bible's teaching about sound doctrine? Several lessons may be suggested.

1. *We must judge between sound doctrine and false doctrine.* Whatever is expressly taught in the Bible is true, and whatever is contrary is false. If God expects us to understand His Word (and He does), then He expects us to make this distinction. To deny this is to deny the very difference between truth and falsehood. It makes the Bible's condemnation of false doctrine meaningless. Part of the duty of the elders is to refute those who contradict sound doctrine, and to "reprove them severely that they may be sound in the faith" (Titus 1:9, 13). Judging a doctrine to be false expresses love for the truth (2 Thessalonians 2:10), love for the church (Acts 20:28-30), and love for the one in error.

2. *Faith in certain doctrines is a condition for salvation and fellowship.* The distinction between essentials and non-essentials has long been recognized. Accepting certain items of faith is essential for salvation. What are these essentials? It is generally agreed that one must

confess that Jesus is Lord, or that He is the Christ, the Son of the Living God. Is anything more required? Yes, as the next section shows.

3. *Sound doctrine includes not just "express statements" but also the intended and proper meaning of those statements.* A word or statement must not be separated from its meaning as originally intended by its author. If a particular affirmation is essential for salvation, so is the proper understanding of it. If "express statements" are matters of faith, so are the intended meanings of those statements.

Certainly there are differences of opinion and interpretation among faithful believers, many of which need not disturb their fellowship at all. This is true especially where the meaning of a passage is very difficult to discern, or where the issue is of little consequence.

The problem is that some attempt to place *all* interpretations in the category of "personal opinion" and treat them as non-essentials. One writer says that "the only confession of faith anyone has a right to require of a candidate for fellowship" is the confession of Jesus Christ: that He is Lord, or the Christ, or the Son of God. "He need not state his views on the nature of Scripture, atonement, the second coming of Christ or many other important doctrines." Another has said that such items as Biblical inerrancy, Christ's virgin birth, His substitutionary atonement, His bodily resurrection, and His second coming "are not inherent in the Good Confession" that Jesus is the Christ, the Son of the Living God.

Such thinking is unacceptable, however, because it assumes that words can be separated from their meanings. When a writer uses a word or expression, he uses it with a *particular* meaning, which is usually clear enough. This is true of the inspired writers of the Bible.

Is it possible, then, to separate mere affirmations about Jesus from the understanding or interpretations of them? May not certain interpretations be false, even false to the extent that they are virtual *denials* of the Biblical teaching about Christ?

Here are some examples. Chistian Scientists confess Jesus as the Christ, meaning that the principle of Truth animated the man Jesus, enabling Him to cast out error and disease. A modern liberal confesses Jesus as Lord, meaning that He is "the goal or limit toward which human existence tends." Jehovah's Witnesses confess Jesus as Son of God, meaning that He was produced by God as the first created being. In each case, though the *words* are Biblical, the *meanings* attached to them are actually a denial of the teaching of Scripture.

When one confesses Jesus as the Christ, he must mean what Scripture means by it—that Jesus is the promised and anointed Savior whose substitutionary death saves His people from their sins. To confess Jesus as the Son of God, one must mean, as does Scripture, that He is eternal God in the flesh (see John 5:17-47; 10:25-39). To confess Him as Lord is to acknowledge His victory over death in His bodily resurrection (Romans 10:9, 10), and His second coming when His lordship will be revealed to all (Philippians 2:11; Revelation 19:16).

One may not understand all that is involved in the confession when he first makes it, but he certainly cannot consciously *deny* any aspect of its meaning. To deny the intended meaning is to deny the fact.

4. *Sound doctrine is important, even when it is not essential to salvation.* Certainly one can be saved without knowing all the truth. Perhaps he can be saved even if he denies some things that are true. But if a doctrine is true, it is a matter of *faith,* not a matter of opinion. It *should* be believed, even if such belief is not a condition of salvation. It is an "important truth," even if it is not a test of fellowship. *It matters* whether one's doctrine is sound or not.

5. *Doctrines that are not tests of fellowship may still be tests of leadership.* To deny this is to deny the concept of

Christian growth, and the difference between spiritual infancy and maturity. Elders must be "holding fast the faithful word which is in accordance with the teaching" (Titus 1:9). How can they perform their duty of refuting false doctrine if they themselves are in error? This is especially true of such serious errors as the denial of Biblical inerrancy, the acceptance of the doctrine of evolution, the endorsement of present-day miraculous gifts. How this is applied, of course, is up to the individual local congregation; but every leader should know and love truth.

One thing is clear: if we are serious about our submission to the Bible's authority, we must act responsibly with regard to sound doctrine.

12

Instruction in Righteousness

Psalm 119:9-16, 33-40; Hebrews 8:6-8, 13

The Bible is our all-sufficient rule of faith and *practice*. As 2 Timothy 3:16 says, it is profitable "for reproof, for correction, for training in righteousness." It tells us how we should act, how we ought to live. It provides the basis for every moral decision; it instructs us concerning what is right and what is wrong.

Most Christians realize that the Bible *is* the final authority in matters of conduct, but many are not quite sure how to *use* it as such. In this chapter we will concentrate mostly on principles for using the Bible in making ethical decisions.

Choosing a Norm

How does anyone decide which actions are right and which are wrong? *On what basis* does one make such decisions?

Many have thought that human reason alone is sufficient to determine right from wrong. That is, if one would just sit down and think it through very carefully, surely he would recognize that certain actions ought to be done and others avoided. This has been the approach of philosophers for thousands of years. The only trouble is that these philosophers, all using the same powers of reason, have never been able to agree on a uniform standard of conduct.

In today's world a common idea is that there is no single objective norm that applies equally to everyone. Many are saying that each person should simply judge for himself what is right for him. As a high-school senior declared, "If we are going to have morals, let's have personal ones. People should make their own rules."

Even if this were true, we would still have to ask, *on what basis* will one decide? The common answer today is that something down inside you will just tell you if an act is right or wrong. As one writer said, "Mostly my 'stands' are formed by a gut feeling that tells me 'This is Right' or 'This is Wrong.' " An English reader designed for college freshmen put it this way: "Moral is what you feel good after." Others follow the old adage, "Always let your conscience be your guide," as if the conscience were some infallible inner authority on ethics.

Many people never stop to think about the mechanics of ethical decision-making. They just unconsciously absorb the norms (or anti-norms) of our media and culture in general. The moral standards promoted on TV, for instance, become implanted in the uncritical mind and are unconsciously followed. (This is no doubt how the "gut feelings" and "consciences" of many persons are programmed.)

If this is the way morality is to be decided, namely, if it is subjective and relative, then let us be ready to accept the consequences: (1) There will never be general agreement on ethical norms. (2) We will never be able to condemn *anyone*—a rapist, a sadist, a Hitler—for doing what his "gut feelings" tell him is right. (3) In the end, conduct will be determined by the most powerful bully: "might makes right."

Is this the way it has to be? Is this the only way ethical decisions can be made? It is—*if there is no God who has spoken His Word.* As one Dostoyevsky character says, "If there is no God, then everything is permitted."

But this is precisely the point: There is a God, and God has spoken! He has given us an objective, universal, absolute norm for conduct: the Bible. This makes every appeal to some inward, subjective "feeling" invalid. Not even a well-intentioned Christian's appeal to the "inner guidance of the Holy Spirit" is valid. The Spirit does *not* guide us from the inside, but from the outside, through the objectively-recorded Word that He inspired.

The Bible *is* the final authority in matters of conduct, but we must make a conscious choice to submit to its authority. Unless we consciously go to Scripture, we will most likely absorb the prevailing morals and standards of our culture. Understanding this point is vitally important to all, but exceedingly so to parents who are responsible for training up their children in the way of the Lord.

Rightly Dividing the Word

Even though it is no longer the preferred translation of 2 Timothy 2:15, the concept of "rightly dividing the word of truth" is extremely important for decision-making. We must know how the different parts of the Bible apply to our present situation.

Of basic importance is the historical distinction between the old-covenant age and the new-covenant age. The focal point of the Bible and of history itself is the work of Jesus Christ, especially His death and resurrection. God began the historical preparation for this as soon as sin entered the world (Genesis 3:15). The major factor in this preparation was the selection and long cultivation of the nation of Israel. Through His special association with this one nation, God developed the proper context for the coming of Christ.

God's unique relationship with Israel is called the "old covenant." This included a special set of laws that helped to maintain a context of holiness and godliness, and that also pointed ahead to the work of Christ. There was also a body of prophetic revelation that built up within Israel the strong expectation of a coming Savior. Thus when Christ came, He came to a (relatively) godly people who were expecting Him.

It is important for us to see that under the old covenant, everything that God was doing in relation to Israel was *preparation* for the first coming of Christ. This is especially true of the law of Moses, with regard to the ceremonies and ordinances that regulated the religious and community life of the Israelites. Much if not most of the Mosaic law applied *only* to this particular nation in their preparatory role. After Jesus came and accomplished His work, the old covenant was set aside. Israel's unique relation to God was abolished, along with all the detailed rituals and social regulations. See Ephesians 2:11-22 and the whole book of Hebrews.

Since Christ's historical work was not completed until His resurrection, the old covenant was still in force throughout most of the life and ministry of Jesus. This is why, even in the Gospel records, people were still obeying the law of Moses.

With the death of Jesus, a new covenant was established, one that applies to *all* nations, including Israelites. Those of us who acknowledge the new covenant and seek to live it are the church, or God's *new* Israel. The social and religious laws that were necessary because of national Israel's unique preparatory role no longer apply. The only commands from the Old Testament that apply to the church are those that reflect God's eternal moral law, those that state principles and rules that are *always* and *everywhere* valid, just because God is God. Even though they were uttered while the old covenant was still in effect, the teachings of Jesus in the Gospels also apply, since He was giving instructions for His new people, the church. Of course the rest of the New Testament applies to the church as well.

Thus when we as Christians seek to determine what is right and wrong for us today, our basic resource is the New Testament, along with the eternally valid moral principles from the Old Testament (which are usually repeated in the New Testament anyway).

A further word needs to be said about the use of the New Testament itself. It is commonly believed that some parts of it are more authoritative than others. Many think that the teachings of Jesus (sometimes printed in red) have some kind of authority that surpasses the rest of the New Testament. This is not so. The Sermon on the Mount, for instance, has no more authority than Romans or 1 Peter, because the whole New Testament comes ultimately from Jesus through the Holy Spirit. See John 16:13-15.

We should also note that the *life* and *example* of Jesus carry no greater weight than the rest of the New Testament. In fact, at many points His life is *not* an example for us, nor was it intended to be. His mission was unique. Jesus did not come to earth simply to show us how to live a perfect life. He came to die for our sins, and His perfect life was necessary for His perfect sacrifice. To look at Jesus merely as an ethical example misses the whole point of His obedience.

Thus we see that God's written Word, rightly divided, is the only authoritative norm for right conduct.

Applying General Principles

A few years ago a survey showed that many Protestant ministers consider the Bible irrelevant because "there is little specific guidance in it for specific problems." It is true that the Bible is not a detailed rule book that gives specific instructions for every conceivable issue in all times and places. But rather than being a weakness, this is precisely the Bible's strength and genius: it provides *general principles* that are relevant to *any* age or culture.

Recognizing this fact is one of the most important steps in learning to use the Bible for ethical guidance. Some moral questions are specifically answered. For instance, fornication is expressly condemned (1 Corinthians 6:9-18). In many other cases, however, we are given general principles that we are expected to apply to specific problems honestly, intelligently, and unselfishly.

For instance, underlying the commandment, "You shall not murder" (Exodus 20:13), is the basic principle that human life must be respected in every way because it is created in God's own image. Thus we are obligated to ask concerning anything we do, "Does this show disrespect or disregard for a fellow human being? Does it violate his integrity as one made in God's image?" Thus murder is forbidden (Genesis 9:6), but so is cursing anyone (James 3:9, 10), and hatred (1 John 3:15), and ridicule (Matthew 5:21, 22).

Once we understand that this is the way the Bible is profitable for instruction in righteousness, it becomes very exciting to see how it touches every single area of life. For instance, there is wide application of the Biblical teaching on the purpose of civil government, namely, *justice,* which includes *protecting* the rights of the innocent and *punishing* violaters (Romans 12:17—13:7; 1 Timothy 2:1-4; 1 Peter 2:13, 14). This helps us understand the rationale for capital punishment and defensive warfare. It helps us to know how to vote in elections. It helps us to keep the church from usurping the government's responsibility and vice versa.

Every Christian, especially every preacher or teacher, must work hard to understand the general principles of Scripture and to apply them to everyday decisions. Thus will the Bible come alive with meaning, and we will echo the sentiment of the psalmist, "O how I love thy law! It is my meditation all the day" (Psalm 119:97).

13

The Authority of the Bible

1 Timothy 6:12-16; Matthew 28:18-20
James 1:21-25; Hebrews 6:1-3; Luke 6:46-49

To whom shall we grant the right to rule over us? To
whom shall we submit our minds and wills? Who shall
determine what is true and false? Who shall make the
decisions concerning right and wrong? Who shall have
the final word in our lives?

At stake here is the question of *authority,* which is the
power and right to determine the norm or standard in
matters of truth and conduct, and to command and en-
force conformity with this norm. This is the most basic of
all questions, since all our thinking and all our decisions
depend ultimately upon what we have selected as our
final authority.

The mood of modern man is to reject every authority
external to himself and thus to set himself up as his own
authority. "No one is going to tell *me* what to do," he says
defiantly. "I shall be the final arbiter; I shall decide what
is right for myself."

Against such presumptuous autonomy God declares,
"NO! You shall have no gods except *Me!*" This is where
the Christian stands. We acknowledge God's absolute

right to rule over us; we yield to Him in unconditional surrender. We acknowledge, too, that God exercises his authority over us *in the person of Jesus Christ and through His Word.* This is the point that must be made in this final chapter.

Jesus Is Lord

In the Bible two people are specifically named as having made the good confession. One was Timothy (1 Timothy 6:12), but in his case we do not know its circumstances or its content. The other was Jesus himself, who made the good confession "before Pontius Pilate" (1 Timothy 6:13). What was the nature of His confession? He declared His kingship or lordship. See John 18:37; 1 Timothy 6:14-16.

Following this example, the church's "good confession" always was and continues to be "Jesus is Lord!" When confronted by the risen Christ, believing Thomas could only cry, "My Lord and my God!" (John 20:28). The same faith and the same confession are required of all who would receive salvation: "If you confess with your mouth Jesus as Lord, and believe in your heart that God raised Him from the dead, you shall be saved" (Romans 10:9). The indwelling Spirit will enable the Christian to make this confession even under severe persecution (1 Corinthians 12:3). His exalted nature and state make it fitting "that every tongue should confess that Jesus Christ is Lord" (Philippians 2:11).

When the Christian makes this confession, as he continues to do throughout his life, what is he saying *about Jesus?* The basic meaning of the original Greek word for *Lord* is "owner" (as in our word *landlord).* Thus we are saying that Jesus is the *owner* of the entire universe. He is the owner because even before He became a man, when He existed as the eternal and divine Word, He created everything that had a beginning (John 1:1-3). He is owner also because in His death and resurrection as a man, He met and conquered His enemies and thus gained the world as the spoils of victory (Matthew 28:18; Revelation 1:18). Because He is Creator and Victor, He is Lord, having absolute authority over all things.

When we as Christians confess Jesus as Lord, we are also saying something *about ourselves*. We are acknowledging that Jesus is *our* Lord, *our* owner. This is our confession of the absolute authority of Jesus over our lives. We are confessing ourselves to be His bondservants, His willing slaves (Philippians 1:1). In unconditional surrender we are saying, "Not my will, but thine be done." "Have thine own way, *Lord.*"

In the person of Jesus of Nazareth God himself has entered the world. The full measure of God's being and authority rests upon Him (Colossians 2:9), and we yield ourselves to every claim that God has on us when we say, "Jesus is Lord."

His Word Is Final

Anyone who has a measure of authority exercises it through his words. This is the natural and effective way for authority to be expressed. For example, who can forget the ringing authority of Pharaoh's words in the movie "The Ten Commandments" when he said, "So let it be written; so let it be done!" The person in authority determines what shall be done and verbalizes it in an edict or command.

This is precisely the manner in which Jesus exercises His lordship: through His Word. That He *is* Lord of the universe and of our lives would mean nothing at all if He did not make His will available to us through His Word. This He has done through the Bible. The New Testament revelation in particular—*all* of it—is Christ's own teaching. See John 16:12-15. This is how He expresses His will.

Since Scripture is God's own Word, the New Testament in particular being the Word of Christ, it speaks to us with God's own authority. The authority of the

New Testament is the very authority of Christ himself. *There is absolutely no difference between the personal authority of Jesus Christ and the authority of His Word, the Bible,* as some would have us think. We do not have to choose between the authority of Christ and the authority of the Bible. They are exactly the same thing.

Picture a young man who says, "Dad, I respect and honor your authority." His father says, "Good! I was just going to tell you to clean your room and take out the garbage." The orders are ignored, however; so the father asks angrily, "You said you respect my authority! Are you now denying it and rebelling against it?" The lad answers, "No, I still accept your authority." The father replies, "But you didn't do what I said!" The reply comes, "Oh, that was just your command, your *word.* I submit to *you* and your personal authority, but not necessarily to your *word.*" This is obviously ridiculous, and so is any attempt to separate the authority of Christ from the authority of *His* Word, the Bible.

The Bible has authority at all *only because* it is the inspired and inerrant Word of God. If it is not His Word, it has *no* authority; but if it *is* His Word—and it is—then it speaks with His very own authority.

How, then, do we demonstrate our submission to Christ's lordship? Only by our absolute, unconditional surrender to the teachings of His Word. We must accept its truth as binding upon our minds, and its rules as binding upon our wills and conduct. "Loyal to Christ and every teaching of His Word"—there is no other way! His Word is final!

A person's true attitude toward Jesus is reflected in his attitude toward Scripture. How can a Christian say, "I know that's what the Bible says, but I don't care"? Saying "Jesus is Lord" and defying the Bible is inconsistent, hypocritical, and rebellious. This accusation comes from Jesus himself: "And why do you call me, 'Lord, Lord,' and do not do what I say?" (Luke 6:46).

If Jesus is Lord, His Word is *final*. We must let it *be* the final authority in our lives and churches, in every matter of faith and practice.

Bible Knowledge Is Imperative

If surrender to Christ as Lord means submission to His Word, then Bible knowledge is imperative. How can Jesus exercise His lordship over us through His Word if we do not *know* His Word? This is why Bible knowledge must be one of the highest priorities in the church program generally and in the life of the individual Christian.

All would agree that the average Christian's Bible knowledge is far below what it should be. What can the church do to bring about a revolution in this critical area? Several things may be suggested.

1. The local eldership must take the lead in emphasizing Bible knowledge. They must see that the church's overall program is geared to accomplish this purpose. They must also be serious about growing in their own personal understanding of Scripture. Why should not a Bible college and/or seminary education be the goal of every *elder*? Paying the necessary tuition would be a good investment for any local church.

2. Ministers must resolve to make Bible knowledge their primary area of expertise. This should include intense preparation, including training at the seminary level. It should also include continuing study, not just in froth but in solid Biblical materials. Churches should encourage such study, providing a book allowance and time off for special seminary work.

3. Bible exposition and Bible doctrine should be the main content of all teaching and preaching in the church. Special classes can be scheduled during the year. Teacher training must be taken seriously.

4. The use of Bible-study aids and materials must be encouraged. Establish and promote a church library. Recommend reference works for each family to own.

Give brief book reviews in the church paper. Avoid frothy, subjective, experiential materials.

5. The churches *must* give more active support to Bible colleges and seminaries. This includes financial support from the church budget. (A church that fails to support the Bible colleges and seminaries is like a farmer who never fertilizes his soil, but just keeps *taking* from it and *taking* from it, never giving back to it, until it is no longer able to provide what he needs.) Churches and Christian parents must encourage *every* Christian youth to attend Bible college for at least one or two years, regardless of his ultimate vocational goal.

Though Bible knowledge is imperative, it is not an end in itself. It is merely the starting point, the basis on which we build our fellowship, our worship, our love (1 Timothy 1:5). Its ultimate goal is full submission to the lordship of Christ.

Jesus said that everyone who hears His words and acts upon them is like a wise man who builds his house upon a rock (Matthew 7:24). The rock is Christ *and* His Word, the Bible. Scripture is *solid*. Let us build upon it.